I0018797

Applications of AI & ML Across Industries

By

Mr. Rakesh Densel

Copyright © 2025 Mr. Rakesh Densel

All rights reserved.

ISBN: 979-82-808551-6-8

Dedication

To my dearest patient, whose strength taught me
resilience.
To my loving spouse, whose unwavering support lights
my path.
And to my friends, who believed in me when it mattered
most.
This book is as much yours as it is mine.

Preface

Applications of AI & ML Across Industries offers a comprehensive exploration into the expansive domain of artificial intelligence (AI) and machine learning (ML). Designed to bridge the gap between theoretical understanding and practical application, this book reveals how these transformative technologies are revolutionising a multitude of industries. Organised for a progressive learning journey, it begins with foundational definitions and core concepts, and then moves into a historical overview that traces the evolution and growing significance of AI and ML. Readers will gain insight into various types of machine learning and the nuanced, interconnected relationship between AI and ML, underlining their role as key drivers of modern innovation.

In healthcare, AI and ML are redefining diagnostics and treatment planning, enabling faster and more accurate patient care. In parallel, the business and finance sectors are undergoing digital transformation through enhanced customer engagement, robust fraud prevention systems, and intelligent algorithmic trading. The development of autonomous systems—including self-driving vehicles, drones, and smart infrastructure—further illustrates the profound influence of these technologies on everyday life.

A dedicated focus on Natural Language Processing (NLP) delves into cutting-edge advancements in speech recognition, text analysis, and conversational AI, showing how machines are learning to communicate with humans in increasingly sophisticated ways. In the manufacturing sector, AI-driven predictive maintenance, real-time quality control, and intelligent production lines are streamlining operations and boosting efficiency. Meanwhile, the entertainment and media landscape are being reshaped through AI's role in content recommendation, video editing, interactive gaming, and sentiment analysis, showcasing its creative and analytical potential.

By integrating practical insights and real-world case studies, **Applications of AI & ML Across Industries** empowers readers to grasp and apply these technologies with confidence. Whether you're a student, industry professional, or curious enthusiast, this book is an invaluable guide for understanding how AI and ML can be harnessed to drive innovation and tackle real-world challenges.

Table of Content

vi

Acknowledgments

I would like to express my heartfelt gratitude to everyone who stood by me throughout the creation of this book.

To my **spouse**, thank you for your unwavering support, patience, and encouragement during every late night and early morning spent writing.

To my **friends**, your constant motivation and belief in my abilities kept me going even when the path wasn't easy.

A special thanks to my **patient**, whose strength and determination inspired me more than words can say.

I'm also grateful to the **technical community** and tools that made my research and writing smoother, and to the countless developers, writers, and innovators who continue to shape the world of AI and ML.

Lastly, I thank **you, the reader**, for choosing this book. May it inspire you to explore, learn, and grow in the fascinating world of Artificial Intelligence and Machine Learning.

CHAPTER 1

An Overview of AI and ML

Learning Objective

This chapter introduces the foundational definitions and key concepts of AI and ML, tracing their history and evolution, exploring various types of machine learning, distinguishing between AI and ML, and highlighting their importance in modern technology.

1.1 Definitions and Key Concepts

Artificial Intelligence (AI) and Machine Learning are frequently applied interchangeably; however, machine learning is a subset of the more comprehensive category of AI.

Artificial intelligence is the general capacity of computers to simulate human thought and execute tasks in real-world settings, while machine learning encompasses the technologies and algorithms that allow systems to recognise patterns, make decisions, and enhance themselves through data and experience.

1. Definition of Artificial Intelligence (AI)

"Artificial intelligence is a field of science concerned with building computers and machines that can reason, learn, and act

in such a way that would normally require human intelligence or that involves data whose scale exceeds what humans can analyse."

AI is a broad field that encompasses many different disciplines, including computer science, data analytics and statistics, hardware and software engineering, linguistics, neuroscience, and even philosophy and psychology.

2. Core Concepts in AI

The fundamental concepts and technologies of AI are what allow machines to execute tasks that ordinarily necessitate human intelligence. The following are a few fundamental concepts:

a. **Machine Learning (ML)**: This serves as the foundation of artificial intelligence, as algorithms acquire knowledge from data without resorting to explicit programming. It entails using a data set to train an algorithm, which enables it to become better over time and make judgements or predictions based on fresh data.

b. **Neural Networks**: In the disciplines of AI, machine learning, and deep learning, these networks of algorithms are inspired by the human brain and replicate the manner in which neurones interact. This enables computers to identify patterns and resolve common issues.

c. **Deep Learning**: Deep learning is a subset of machine learning that employs sophisticated neural networks with numerous layers (hence the term "deep") to analyse a variety of data factors. This is essential for tasks such as speech and image recognition.

d. **Natural Language Processing (NLP)**: Natural Language Processing is the process of programming computers to process and analyse large quantities of natural language data, thereby facilitating interactions between humans and computers that utilise natural language.

e. **Robotics**: Robotics, which is frequently linked to artificial intelligence, combines AI concepts with physical components to develop devices that are capable of executing a diverse range of tasks, including intricate operations and assembly lines.

f. **Cognitive Computing**: This AI method typically employs data mining, pattern recognition, and NLP to solve intricate problems by imitating human brain processes.

g. **Expert Systems**: These are artificial intelligence systems that replicate the decision-making capabilities of a human expert, utilising reasoning capabilities to arrive at conclusions.

Each of these ideas contributes to the development of systems that may improve, automate, and sometimes surpass human performance in certain activities.

3. Definition of Machine Learning (ML)

"Machine Learning (ML) is a discipline of Artificial Intelligence (AI) that provides machines with the ability to automatically

3

learn from data and past experiences while identifying patterns to make predictions with minimal human intervention."

4. Concepts of Machine Learning

A few basic concepts of machine learning are as follows:

a) Data

Data serves as the basic building block of machine learning. The algorithm would be unable to learn without data. Structured data, such as spreadsheets and databases, and unstructured data, such as text and images, are among the numerous forms of data that can be encountered. One of the most important aspects that may greatly affect the machine learning algorithm's effectiveness is the amount and quality of the data used to train it.

b) Feature

The variables or attributes that are employed to describe the input data in machine learning are referred to as features. To enable the algorithm to make precise predictions or decisions, the objective is to identify the most pertinent and informative features. In the machine learning process, feature selection is an essential stage, as the algorithm's performance is significantly influenced by the quality and relevance of the features employed.

c) Model

A mathematical representation of the connection between the input data (features) as well as the output (predictions or judgements) is called a machine learning model. A training dataset is employed to construct the model, which is subsequently assessed using a distinct validation dataset. The objective is to develop a model that is capable of accurately generalising to previously unseen data.

d) Training

The process of educating a machine learning algorithm to generate precise predictions or decisions is known as training. This is accomplished by supplying the algorithm with a substantial dataset and enabling it to learn from the patterns and relationships present in the data. The algorithm modifies its internal parameters during the training process to reduce the discrepancy between its predicted and actual output.

e) Testing

The machine learning algorithm's performance is assessed on a distinct dataset that it has not encountered previously through the process of testing. The objective is to ascertain the extent to which the algorithm generalises to previously unseen data. Upon satisfactory performance on the assessment dataset, the algorithm is deemed to be an effective model.

f) Overfitting

Overfitting is a phenomenon that arises when a machine learning model is excessively intricate and closely approximates the training data. This can result in subpar performance on new, unobserved data due to the model's overspecialisation on the training dataset. To preclude overfitting, it is crucial to assess the model's performance using a validation dataset and to streamline the model using regularisation techniques.

g) Underfitting

Underfitting is a phenomenon that arises when a machine learning model is overly simplistic and is unable to accurately represent the patterns and relationships present in the data. This may result in poor performance on the testing and training datasets. It is possible to prevent underfitting by employing a variety of techniques, including feature engineering, reducing regularisation, collecting additional data, and increasing model complexity.

1.2 History and Evolution of AI and ML

The history and evolution of artificial intelligence and machine learning are characterised by significant progress and innovative breakthroughs. Artificial intelligence has evolved into an intriguing and irrepressible discipline, from its initial theoretical concepts to its current implementations in a variety of sectors.

1.2.1 History and Evolution of AI

The concept of "artificial intelligence" has roots that extend back thousands of years, originating from ancient philosophers who pondered questions surrounding life and death. In ancient times, there were creations known as "automatons," which were mechanical devices that operated without the need for human control. The term "automaton" has its origins in ancient Greek, signifying "acting of one's own will." A record from 400 BCE mentions a mechanical pigeon made by a companion of the philosopher Plato, marking one of the earliest instances of an automaton. Years later, one of the most renowned automatons was crafted by Leonardo da Vinci circa 1495.

1. Groundwork for AI 1900-1950:

During the early 1900s, a significant amount of media was produced that focused on the concept of artificial humans. Scientists from various fields began to enquire whether it was feasible to develop an artificial brain. Certain creators developed various iterations of what is now referred to as "robots," a term that originated from a Czech play in 1921, although the majority of these creations were quite basic. Most of these were powered by steam, and a few could make facial expressions and even walk.

    a. **1921:** Czech playwright Karel Čapek released a science fiction play titled "Rossum's Universal Robots," which introduced the concept of "artificial people" that he referred to as robots. The initial recorded instance of the term occurred at this time.

    b. **1929:** The first Japanese robot, named Gakutensoku, was built by professor Makoto Nishimura.

c. **1949:** Edmund Callis Berkley, a computer scientist, published a book titled "Giant Brains, or Machines that Think," in which he drew comparisons between the latest computer models and human brains.

2. Birth of AI: 1950-1956

This period marked a peak in the interest surrounding AI. Alan Turing's work titled "Computer Machinery and Intelligence" was published, leading to the development of The Turing Test, a tool utilised by experts to assess computer intelligence. The phrase "artificial intelligence" was created and gained widespread recognition.

a. **1950:** Alan Turing published a work titled "Computer Machinery and Intelligence," in which he introduced a test for machine intelligence known as The Imitation Game.

b. **1952:** A computer scientist by the name of Arthur Samuel created a program capable of playing checkers, marking it as the first to learn the game on its own.

c. **1955:** A workshop was held at Dartmouth by John McCarthy on the topic of "artificial intelligence," marking the first instance of the term's usage and its journey into popular culture.

3. AI Maturation: 1957-1979

The period from the creation of the phrase "artificial intelligence" to the 1980s was marked by both significant advancements and challenges in AI research. The period from the late 1950s to the 1960s was marked by a surge of creativity. The evolution of programming languages that remain relevant today, alongside literature and cinema that delved into the concept of robots, contributed to the rapid emergence of AI as a mainstream notion.

During the 1970s, notable advancements occurred, including the construction of the first anthropomorphic robot in Japan and the development of the first autonomous vehicle by an engineering graduate student. Nonetheless, it was also a period marked by challenges for AI research.

4. AI Boom: 1980-1987

The 1980s were characterised by a significant surge in growth and enthusiasm for AI, which is now referred to as the "AI boom." Both breakthroughs in research and increased government funding contributed to supporting the researchers. Techniques in Deep Learning and the application of Expert Systems gained popularity, enabling computers to learn from errors and make autonomous decisions.

   a. **1980:** The initial expert system entered the commercial market, referred to as XCON (expert configurer). To facilitate the procurement of computer systems, it was developed to autonomously select components that align with the customer's requirements.

b. **1985:** A demonstration of an autonomous drawing program called AARON takes place at the AAAI conference.

c. **1986:** The first driverless car, also known as a robot car, was created and demonstrated by Ernst Dickmann and his team at Bundeswehr University of Munich. The vehicle was capable of reaching speeds of up to 55 mph on roads free from obstacles or other drivers.

d. **1987:** Alactrious Inc. has initiated the commercial launch of Alacrity. The first strategic management advice system, Alacrity, used a sophisticated expert system with more than 3,000 rules.

5. AI Winter: 1987-1993

The "Association for the Advancement of Artificial Intelligence (AAAI)" issued a warning, and an AI Winter arrived. This period is characterised by diminished interest from consumers, the public, and private sectors in AI, resulting in reduced research funding and consequently fewer breakthroughs.

Interest in AI waned among private investors and the government, leading to a cessation of funding as a result of high costs compared to perceived low returns. The AI Winter occurred due to various setbacks in the machine market and expert systems, such as the conclusion of the Fifth Generation project, reductions in strategic computing initiatives, and a deceleration in the implementation of expert systems.

6. AI Agents: 1993-2011

The early 90s demonstrated significant advancements in AI research, highlighted by the emergence of the first AI system capable of defeating a reigning world champion chess player. This era marked the introduction of AI into daily life through innovations like the initial Roomba and the first speech recognition software available for Windows computers.

In response to the increase in interest, there was a subsequent increase in research funding, which facilitated even further advancements.

a. **1997:** Deep Blue, created by IBM, defeated the world chess champion, Gary Kasparov, in a widely publicised match, marking the first time a program triumphed over a human chess champion.

b. **1997:** A speech recognition software was released by Windows, which was developed by Dragon Systems.

c. **2000:** The first robot capable of simulating human emotions through facial features, such as eyes, eyebrows, ears, and mouth, was developed by Professor Cynthia Breazeal. The name given to it was Kismet.

d. **2002:** The initial model of the Roomba was launched.

e. **2003:** Two rovers were landed on Mars by NASA, named Spirit and Opportunity, and they explored the planet's surface autonomously.

f. **2006:** Organisations like Twitter, Facebook, and Netflix began incorporating AI into their advertising and user experience algorithms.

g. **2010:** The Xbox 360 Kinect was launched by Microsoft as the first gaming hardware intended to monitor body movement and convert it into gaming commands.

h. **2011:** A computer designed for natural language processing, known as Watson and developed by IBM, triumphed in a televised game of Jeopardy against two previous champions.

i. **2011:** Siri was released by Apple as the first widely recognised virtual assistant.

7. **Artificial Intelligence is Everywhere: 2012 – Present**

This has resulted in the most recent developments in artificial intelligence that are currently in effect. Common-use AI tools, such as search engines and virtual assistants, have experienced a significant increase in popularity. It was during this period that Deep Learning and Big Data gained prominence.

a. **2016:** Hanson Robotics developed Sophia, a humanoid robot that was dubbed the first "robot citizen" and was the first robot to possess the capacity to communicate, see, and replicate emotions, as well as assume a realistic human appearance.

b. **2017:** The two AI chatbots that Facebook programmed were intended to engage in conversation and acquire negotiation skills. However, as they conversed, they ceased to use English and established their own language entirely independently.

c. **2018:** On a Stanford reading comprehension test, the language-processing AI developed by a Chinese tech company named Alibaba outperformed human intelligence.

d. **2019:** AlphaStar, an artificial intelligence developed by Google, achieved Grandmaster status in the video game StarCraft 2, surpassing the performance of all human participants except for 2%.

e. **2020:** OpenAI has initiated beta testing of GPT-3, a model that employs Deep Learning to generate code, poetry, and other language and writing tasks. Despite not being the first of its kind, it is the first to generate content that is nearly indistinguishable from that produced by humans.

f. **2021:** The development of DALL-E by OpenAI has brought AI one step closer to comprehending the visual world by enabling it to process and comprehend images sufficiently to generate precise captions.

g. **2022:** DALL-E was incorporated into ChatGPT to demonstrate the ability of AI to produce images and texts, respectively, igniting interest in new creative opportunities.

h. **2023:** The creation of multimodal models, which are capable of processing data types such as text, images, video, and audio, was a significant AI advancement. Innovations such as OpenAI's GPT and Google DeepMind's Gemini were the driving force behind this trend, which enabled interactions with AI through a variety of methodologies.

i. **2024:** Sora, Open AI's text-to-video model, and Devin, the first AI software engineer.

Generative AI: Generative AI made substantial progress in 2023, as evidenced by the advent of a variety of models, including Meta's LLaMA 2, Google's Bard chatbot, Baidu's Ernie Bot, and OpenAI's GPT-4. Although there was some initial excitement, the year was characterised by a focus on the potential and constraints of generative AI, to incorporate it into practical applications to improve productivity.

Augmented Reality (AR) and Quantum Computing: In 2023, AI was paralleled by substantial advancements in other technologies, including AR and quantum computation. IBM's System Two and Heron quantum semiconductor, as well as AR technologies like Apple's Vision Pro eyewear, have made significant strides in their respective disciplines. This suggests that these technologies may eventually become more incorporated into daily life.

1.2.2 History and Evolution of ML

Machine Learning (ML) has developed from philosophical concepts regarding artificial intelligence into a fundamental technology of the contemporary era. It has undergone numerous phases, from the earliest neural networks to the deep learning models of today. The comprehension of ML's history offers a window into the manner in which it has expanded to influence industries and daily life.

1. The Early Days of Machine Learning

The following explores the early days of machine learning:

a. Philosophical Foundations

It is possible to trace the origins of machine learning to early philosophical concepts. The concept of logical reasoning was introduced by Aristotle, who posited that thought processes could adhere to structured principles, similar to mechanical engineering systems. René Descartes subsequently suggested that machines could potentially replicate certain aspects of human thought, indicating the potential for intelligent systems. The development of AI and ML was impacted by these early theories of logic and reasoning.

b. Early Computational Devices

Machine learning was established by the development of early computational devices. The Analytical Engine, which Charles Babbage developed, and other early machines demonstrated the potential of devices that could conduct intricate calculations. These systems facilitated subsequent advancements in computation and motivated researchers to investigate the potential of machines to learn from data.

c.   The Turing Test (1950)

The Turing Test, which Alan Turing introduced in 1950, assessed a machine's capacity to manifest intelligence similar to that of a human. However, the Turing Test had substantial implications for machine learning, despite its primary focus on AI. It had an impact on subsequent studies of learning algorithms by implying that robots may be trained to react intelligently to input.

d.   First Neural Network (1943)

Warren McCulloch and Walter Pitts introduced the first mathematical model of a neural network in 1943. Their research illustrated the mathematical representation of neurones and the numerical simulation of neural processes by machines. Despite its limitations, this model established the foundation for future developments in neural networks and influenced the early research in machine learning.

2.   Milestones in Machine Learning Development (1950-2000)

The following are the significant milestones in the development of machine learning from 1950 to 2000:

a.   Computer Checkers (1952)

Machine learning was introduced by Arthur Samuel in 1952 when he developed a computer-based checkers program. Samuel's program was developed to enhance its functionality by incorporating lessons from previous games, providing the first practical application of machine learning in the gaming industry. This advancement demonstrated the capacity of machines to learn autonomously, thereby establishing a precedent for future ML applications.

b. The Perceptron (1957)

Frank Rosenblatt introduced the Perceptron in 1957, a single-layer neural network model that is capable of recognising patterns. The Perceptron, developed by Rosenblatt, sparked considerable enthusiasm by illustrating the potential for machines to learn from input data. Nevertheless, the model's limitations were revealed by its incapacity to resolve non-linear problems, such as XOR. This caused discussions about neural network's potential and momentarily halted the field's development.

c. Nearest Neighbour Algorithm (1967)

In 1967, the Nearest Neighbour algorithm was developed, which represented a substantial advancement in the field of pattern recognition.

This technique made it possible for computers to group data points according to how close they were to other points in a dataset. It became an essential instrument for tasks such as clustering and handwriting recognition, demonstrating the expanding potential of ML in practical applications.

d. The Backpropagation Algorithm (1974)

The backpropagation algorithm's introduction in 1974 marked a significant turning point for neural networks. Backpropagation enabled multi-layer networks to acquire knowledge by rectifying errors through feedback loops. This innovation reignited curiosity in neural networks, thereby establishing the groundwork for deep learning and empowering machines to effectively address more intricate issues.

e. The Stanford Cart (1979)

The Stanford Cart was a pioneering initiative in the field of autonomous vehicles. The cart, which was created in 1979, employed ML algorithms to autonomously navigate obstacles in its environment. This initiative illustrated the effectiveness of machine learning in robotics and served as an inspiration for future research on autonomous systems, such as self-driving vehicles.

f. AI Winter

The AI Winter, which commenced in the 1970s and continued into the 1990s, was characterised by a decline in funding and enthusiasm, despite the success of these milestones. Insufficient computational capacity and data availability were among the constraints that early machine learning models encountered. The decline in research activity was further exacerbated by scepticism regarding the practical application of ML and AI. Nevertheless, researchers maintained their work in the background, establishing the foundation for later discoveries.

3. The Rise of Machine Learning (2000 – Present)

The subsequent section delves into the emergence of machine learning during the 20s:

a. Machine Defeats Man in Chess (1997)

In 1997, IBM's Deep Blue achieved a historic victory over the incumbent world chess champion, Garry Kasparov, even though it was technically predating 2000. Machine learning algorithms' capabilities in pattern recognition and decision-making were demonstrated at this event. It established the possibility of machines competing with human intelligence, which rekindled interest in Machine Learning (ML) and Artificial Intelligence (AI).

b. The Torch Software Library (2002)

The development of ML was significantly altered by the publication of Torch, an open-source software library. Torch facilitated the efficient construction of machine learning models by researchers and developers, thereby fostering community-driven innovation. It facilitated the development of other open-source frameworks, such as PyTorch and TensorFlow, which further accelerated research and made machine learning more accessible.

c. Deep Learning Breakthroughs (2006)

Geoffrey Hinton and his team made significant strides in deep learning in 2006, which allowed neural networks to more efficiently process large datasets. Deep learning was established as a potent subset of machine learning as a result of this advance, which enabled substantial enhancements in fields such as computer vision and speech recognition.

d. Google Brain (2011)

The Google Brain initiative was launched to apply machine learning to large-scale systems. Google implemented ML to enhance services, including search engines and advertising platforms, thereby illustrating its capacity to manage vast datasets. This initiative underscored the significance of ML in the automation and efficacy of various industries.

e. DeepFace (2014)

A facial recognition project known as DeepFace was introduced by Facebook in 2014. This project utilised deep learning to accurately identify faces. This technology illustrated the practical implementations of ML in the fields of biometric security and image recognition. It demonstrated the potential of machine learning to improve authentication systems and established the groundwork for future developments in computer vision.

f. ImageNet Challenge (2017)

The ImageNet Challenge was established as a standard for the assessment of machine learning models in the field of computer vision. In 2017, ML systems attained human-level accuracy in object recognition, a significant milestone in the field of ML. ImageNet's achievement underscored the strengths of deep learning and Convolutional Neural Networks (CNNs) in the development of computer vision technologies.

g. Generative AI (2010s Onwards)

Generative AI models, including GPT and DALL-E, have revolutionised the role of ML in creative industries. This model broadens the scope of ML's applications beyond analytics and predictions by generating text, images, and even music. Generative AI has uncovered novel opportunities in industries such as entertainment, design, and content creation.

1.3   Types of Machine Learning

Machine learning encompasses numerous varieties, each with its own unique applications and characteristics. The primary categories of machine learning algorithms include the following:

a. Supervised Machine Learning
b. Unsupervised Machine Learning
c. Semi-Supervised Machine Learning
d. Reinforcement Learning

1. Supervised Machine Learning

A model is trained on a "Labelled Dataset" in the context of supervised learning. Output and input parameters are present in labelled datasets. In Supervised Learning, algorithms acquire the ability to associate inputs with their corresponding correct outputs. The datasets are labelled for both training and validation purposes.

Example: Imagine a situation in which there is a need to create an image classifier that can distinguish between cats and dogs. The algorithm will learn to classify between a dog and a cat when provided with labelled images of both datasets. Upon inputting new images of dogs or cats that have not been encountered previously, the system will utilise the learnt algorithms to predict whether the image depicts a dog or a cat. This explains the functioning of supervised learning, specifically in the context of image classification.

Two primary categories of supervised learning are outlined below:

a) Classification

Classification involves the prediction of categorical target variables that signify distinct classes or labels. For example, determining if emails are spam or not, or forecasting whether a patient is at high risk for heart disease. Classification algorithms are designed to associate input features with one of the established classes.

The following are a few classification algorithms:

- Logistic Regression
- Support Vector Machine

- Random Forest
- Decision Tree
- K-Nearest Neighbours (KNN)
- Naive Bayes

b) Regression

Regression focusses on the prediction of continuous target variables that signify numerical values. For instance, estimating the cost of a home by considering its dimensions, geographical area, and features, or projecting the sales figures of a product. A continuous numerical value is generated by regression algorithms as they acquire the ability to map the input features.

Here are some regression algorithms:

- Linear Regression
- Polynomial Regression
- Ridge Regression
- Lasso Regression
- Decision tree
- Random Forest

2. Unsupervised Machine Learning

Unsupervised learning is a machine learning technique that involves the identification of patterns and relationships in unlabelled data by an algorithm. Unsupervised learning differs from supervised learning in that it does not necessitate the algorithm to be provided with labelled target outputs. Unsupervised learning frequently revolves around the identification of concealed patterns, clusters, or similarities in the data. These findings can be applied to a variety of applications, including data exploration, visualisation, dimensionality reduction, and more. The working of Supervised learning can be easily understood by the below figure 1.1.

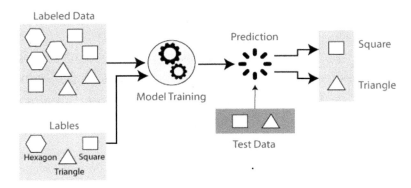

Figure 1.1: Supervised machine learning. [1]

Example: It is important to take into account a dataset that includes details regarding the purchases made from the shop. The algorithm can group similar purchasing behaviours among customers, revealing potential clients without predefined labels through clustering. This kind of information can assist companies in reaching their target customers and recognising outliers.

The following are the two primary categories of

---

[1]https://images.javatpoint.com/tutorial/machine-learning/images/supervised-machine-learning.png

unsupervised learning:

a) Clustering

The process of clustering involves grouping data points into clusters according to their similarity. This technique proves beneficial for recognising patterns and relationships in data without requiring labelled examples.

Some clustering algorithms are presented here:

- K-Means Clustering algorithm
- Mean-shift algorithm
- DBSCAN Algorithm
- Principal Component Analysis
- Independent Component Analysis

b) Association

A technique exists for discovering relationships between items in a dataset, known as association rule learning. According to certain criteria, the existence of one thing indicates the presence of another with a certain probability.

Several algorithms for association rule learning are available:

- Apriori Algorithm
- Eclat
- FP-growth Algorithm

3. Semi-Supervised Learning

Semi-supervised learning is an algorithm that operates in the space between supervised and unsupervised learning, utilising both labelled and unlabelled data. This approach proves to be especially beneficial when acquiring labelled data involves significant costs, time, or resources. This method proves beneficial when dealing with a dataset that requires significant resources and time to manage. Semi-supervised learning is selected when the acquisition of labelled data demands specific skills and appropriate resources for effective training or learning.

These techniques are utilised when dealing with data that has a small number of labelled instances alongside a larger portion that remains unlabelled. Unsupervised techniques can be utilised to predict labels, which can then be provided to supervised techniques. This technique is primarily relevant for image data sets, where it is common for not all images to be labelled (figure 1.2).

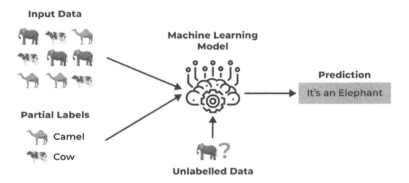

Figure 1.2: Semi-supervised learning. [2]

Example: It is important to recognise that constructing a language translation model requires significant resources when labelled translations for every sentence pair are needed. The models are enabled to learn from both labelled and unlabelled sentence pairs, resulting in increased accuracy. This technique has resulted in notable enhancements in the quality of machine translation services.

A variety of semi-supervised learning methods exist, each possessing unique characteristics. A few of the most frequently encountered examples are:

a) **Graph-based semi-supervised learning:** The relationships between the data points are represented using a graph in this approach. The graph is subsequently employed to propagate labels from the labelled data points to the unlabelled data points.

b) **Label propagation:** The method involves the iterative transfer of labels from labelled data points to unlabelled ones, relying on the similarities observed between the data points.

c) **Co-training:** Two distinct machine learning models are trained on separate subsets of unlabelled data

---

[2]https://media.geeksforgeeks.org/wp-content/uploads/20231123085101/2.png

using this approach. Each model is subsequently utilised to label the predictions made by the other.

d) **Self-training:** The method involves training a machine learning model using labelled data, followed by utilising the model to forecast labels for the unlabelled data. The model undergoes retraining using the labelled data along with the predicted labels for the unlabelled data.

e) **Generative adversarial networks (GANs):** Synthetic data can be produced using GANs, a form of deep learning algorithm. Unlabelled data for semi-supervised learning can be generated using GANs, which involve training a generator and a discriminator as two neural networks.

4. Reinforcement Machine Learning

An approach to learning that engages with the environment by generating actions and identifying mistakes is the reinforcement machine learning algorithm. Delay, trial, and error are the most pertinent attributes of reinforcement learning. This technique involves the model continuously enhancing its performance through Reward Feedback to understand behaviour or patterns.

These algorithms are optimised for specific issues, such as the Google Self-Driving Car and AlphaGo, in which a computer competes with humans and itself to improve its performance in the Go Game. With every instance of data input, the system learns and incorporates the information into its knowledge base, which constitutes the training data. As it learns more, its training improves, leading to greater experience.

Some of the most common algorithms in reinforcement learning include:

a) **Q-learning:** A model-free RL algorithm known as Q-learning learns a Q-function that associates states with actions. The Q-function provides an estimate of the anticipated reward associated with performing a specific action in a certain state.

b) **SARSA (State-Action-Reward-State-Action):** SARSA represents an additional model-free reinforcement learning algorithm that acquires a Q-function. In contrast to Q-learning, SARSA modifies the Q-function based on the action that was performed, instead of the optimal action.

c) **Deep Q-learning:** Deep Q-learning combines Q-learning with deep learning techniques. A neural network is employed to represent the Q-function in deep Q-learning, which enables it to learn intricate relationships between states and actions.

Example: Imagine teaching an AI agent to play a game similar to chess. The agent investigates various actions and obtains either favourable or unfavourable responses depending on the results. Reinforcement learning also discovers applications in which it acquires the ability to execute duties by engaging with its environment (figure 1.3).

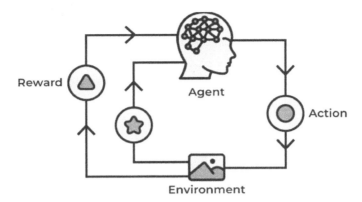

Figure 1.3: Reinforcement Machine Learning. [3]

There are two primary forms of reinforcement learning:

a) **Positive Reinforcement:** It provides a reward to the agent for performing a preferred action. The agent is motivated to replicate the behaviour. For example, awarding a dog a treat for sitting or awarding a point in a game for choosing the correct answer.

b) **Negative Reinforcement:** A desired behaviour is promoted by eliminating an undesirable stimulus. The agent is discouraged from repeating the behaviour. Examples include doing a job to avoid a penalty and turning off a loud alarm when a lever is touched.

1.4 AI vs ML: Key Differences

[3]https://media.geeksforgeeks.org/wp-content/uploads/20231123085353/1-(2).png

The most significant distinction between AI and ML is that the former is a particular technique within the latter. In simpler terms, and as previously mentioned, machine learning is a subset of artificial intelligence that is focused on data-driven learning. Despite their similarities, both technologies possess distinct AI components and represent distinct methodologies within a broader field that enables computers to replicate human intelligence.

ML algorithms are intended to learn patterns and relationships from data to optimise and predict in a rigorously foundational approach. As previously said, generative AI algorithms, on the other hand, concentrate on identifying the underlying structure of the data and producing fresh, lifelike examples that share comparable traits. Several critical distinctions between machine learning and generative AI frequently determine the appropriate timing and method of deployment:

1. Data Requirements

Typically, machine learning algorithms necessitate substantial quantities of labelled data for training. Therefore, each data point must be assigned a corresponding classification or designation. For example, to train a machine learning model for image recognition or speech recognition, a dataset of images or audio samples must be labelled with the desired recognition (e.g., "cat" or "not cat").

Generative AI models may also capitalise on extensive

datasets. However, it is not necessary to assign a designation to the data. All forms of unstructured data can be used to train models to recognise patterns. It remains crucial to bear in mind that the quality and quantity of the data utilised significantly influence the appearance of the outputs that are produced.

2. Processing Capabilities

Primarily, machine learning algorithms are designed to analyse and interpret existing data models. Unlike genAI, they do not strive for a more comprehensive intelligence that is comparable to human cognition and adaptability. This is why they are often exceptional at tasks such as anomaly detection and classification.

In contrast, generative AI algorithms are more effective at generating novel and original data formats. Primarily, they are designed to emulate human behaviour by acquiring abilities that are comparable to those of humans. They are thus often used for the following tasks:

- Generating product designs
- Creating realistic simulations
- Composing novel music pieces
- Editing complex images
- Crafting text content from scratch

3. Desired Outcomes

ML is predominantly an outcome-oriented field. This

objective is to optimise a particular undertaking, such as maximising accuracy or minimising error. To satisfy predetermined performance metrics, machine learning models are trained to generate predictions or decisions from input data.

The fundamental objective of generative AI is to generate an entity that is comparable to the data upon which it was trained, but not identical. Rather than focussing on how well generative AI models perform on particular tasks, the quality and variety of the samples they produce are often used to gauge their effectiveness.

4. Application Scope

Machine learning algorithms are advantageous in numerous domains, including spam filtering and object recognition, which enable data classification. Regression is an additional strength of machine learning, and it can be employed to address a diverse array of prediction and decision-making tasks. Machine learning is a very useful tool in domains like these because of these application cases:

- Healthcare
- Finance
- Marketing
- Autonomous systems

Functions that necessitate "image synthesis, text generation, music composition, and other comparable tasks" are more applicable to generative AI. Generational AI has a wide range of applications in data augmentation and creative industries as a result.

5. Training Paradigm

Supervised or unsupervised learning paradigms are typically employed by ML models contingent upon the objectives. In order to comprehend the correlation between input and output, it is imperative to have access to explicit data examples that include either responses or feedback. The ML training process entails the modification of model parameters to reduce the disparity between the predicted and actual outcomes, as determined by a predetermined loss function of the model.

Models of generative AI frequently depend on self-supervised or unsupervised learning methods. To enhance the quality of the samples they generate, they may also implement adversarial training methods, including GANs, which involve competition between two neural networks.

6. Handling Uncertainty

Machine learning algorithms frequently generate probabilistic predictions or point estimates from the input data. These algorithms are designed to optimise predictive accuracy, minimise prediction errors, and reduce AI bias within the specified uncertainty bounds. It necessitates a greater degree of structure to achieve the anticipated outcomes, as it is more data-driven.

Uncertainty is celebrated as an inherent component of the creative process in generative AI. Therefore, generative AI models are capable of generating a variety of spontaneous and diverse outputs, each with a unique level of novelty. This feature facilitates the exploration and creativity of the samples that are produced, as well as prevents them from appearing identically each time.

7. Interpretability and Explainability

The design of ML models frequently involves the inclusion of features that influence the model's decisions and the ability of users to comprehend and articulate the process of making predictions. The importance of this feature is particularly evident when regulatory compliance and transparency are paramount.

Generative AI models, on the other hand, may forego interpretability in favour of complexity and creativity. The importance of ensuring that these models are comprehensible and reliable for consumers has grown as they progress. In this way, they ensure that the content and AI applications they generate are both relatable and dependable.

1.5   Importance of AI and ML in Modern Technology

Systems and control engineering optimisation has been fuelled by developments in AI and ML in recent years. In the current era of big data, AI and ML can analyse enormous quantities of data in real-time, thereby enhancing the efficacy and accuracy of data-driven decision-making processes. For example, in control engineering, AI algorithms can anticipate system behaviours and automatically modify controls to enhance performance, thereby enhancing reliability and efficiency.

ML models can dynamically adapt to changing environments and operational conditions by continuously improving their predictions and decisions as they process more data, which is facilitated by their learning capabilities. This rapid adaptation enhances the capabilities of current systems and enables the creation of innovative solutions, including autonomous vehicles and smart infrastructures that were previously deemed impractical.

1. Deep Learning and Neural Networks

Neural networks with numerous layers are employed in deep learning, a subset of machine learning, to analyse a variety of data types. These sophisticated algorithms are capable of identifying patterns that conventional algorithms may overlook, and they are particularly adept at processing and interpreting vast datasets. Advancements in fields such as natural language processing (NLP) and image recognition are facilitated by deep learning.

"Convolutional Neural Networks (CNNs) and Recurrent

Neural Networks (RNNs)" are two significant developments in the field of deep learning. The widespread use of CNNs in image recognition systems is due to their ability to effortlessly parse visual information. Breaking down images into components and analysing them layer by layer to identify patterns and features, they replicate the manner in which the human brain processes information. RNNs are optimally adapted for NLP tasks due to their ability to comprehend sequential data. They possess the ability to recall previous inputs in the data sequence, which enables them to employ predictive analytics to generate contextually informed text—a critical component of speech recognition and the production of human language.

Numerous AI innovations are the result of these two emerging technologies. Deep learning is a powerful tool in the field of image and facial recognition technology, enabling computers to accurately identify objects, features, and scenes with the same precision as human perception. This technique has a wide range of applications, including medical imaging diagnostics and surveillance. The development of applications that comprehend, interpret, and produce human speech and language has been facilitated by deep learning in natural language processing. NLP is responsible for the development of conversational AI, translation services, and voice recognition systems.

2.   Reinforcement Learning and Autonomous Systems

Reinforcement Learning (RL) enables devices or software, which are frequently abbreviated as "agents," to acquire the ability to make decisions through trial and error. An agent engages in this process by interacting with its surroundings, behaving, and getting feedback in the form of incentives or sanctions. Essentially, the agent learns from its experiences in a manner similar to that of human beings, optimising its actions to maximise cumulative rewards over time.

Reinforcement learning is implemented in real-world scenarios, particularly in the context of autonomous driving vehicles and robotics. During navigation, RL algorithms in self-driving vehicles analyse a variety of sensory data inputs to make real-time decisions. These algorithms enable autonomous robots to learn how to manipulate objects or navigate environments independently, enabling them to adapt to new tasks through interaction in the field of robotics.

The proliferation of autonomous AI systems has prompted substantial ethical concerns. In situations involving human safety, the delegation of significant decisions to machines presents dilemmas regarding accountability, privacy, and job displacement. Ensuring that these systems make ethical judgements, free from biases that are ingrained in their training data, is a significant challenge. Engineers must adopt a balanced approach when developing these systems, taking into account the ethical implications and their transformative potential to guarantee that they are beneficial to society as a whole.

3. Natural Language Processing Advancements

RNNs are the driving force behind NLP. NLP has revolutionised the manner in which machines comprehend and engage with human language. These advancements are responsible for the creation of chatbots and conversational AI, which facilitate more intuitive and human-like interactions with digital systems. In addition to facilitating transactions, sophisticated NLP models enable programs to comprehend, generate, and engage in conversations with users, thereby providing assistance and accumulating information.

Language barriers are being dismantled worldwide through the application of NLP. Deep learning is employed by contemporary translation models to generate translations that are precise and accurately represent the context and subtleties of the original text. Another frequently employed application of NLP is sentiment analysis, which enables machines to interpret and categorise opinions derived from text data. Businesses may benefit from this by learning important things about the opinions and sentiments of their customers.

The development of NLP is also a driving force behind voice recognition technology. Virtual assistants, such as Siri, Alexa, and Google Assistant, are now capable of comprehending and responding to voice commands, despite the fact that they were previously solely represented in science fiction. The practical applications of these devices include the ability to control smart home devices and set reminders, thereby increasing the accessibility and interactions of technology.

4. Explainable AI and Model Interpretability

Model interpretability and explainable AI (XAI) contribute to the necessity of transparency and comprehension in the decision-making processes of artificial intelligence. The complexity of AI models, especially deep learning networks, has made their decision-making processes seem like "black boxes," meaning that no one can fully comprehend how they function. The developers of XAI are striving to render these processes transparent to enable humans to effectively manage, trust, and comprehend the results of AI.

People are interested in the decision-making process of AI models since they may have major repercussions in autonomous driving and sectors like healthcare and finance. Humans can have confidence that AI decisions are fair, impartial, and consistent with ethical standards as a result of the insights provided by XAI into the underlying reasoning.

Nevertheless, there is a significant tradeoff between the interpretability, accuracy, and complexity of the model. Although highly complex models, such as deep neural networks, frequently obtain superior performance, they are less interpretable. Decision trees and other simpler models are easier to understand, but they don't have the same advanced predictive power as their more complicated counterparts. The model's intended application, the significance of its conclusions, and the need for openness must all be carefully considered to strike a balance between interpretability and accuracy. Implementing post-hoc analytic tools to explain complicated model outputs and creating models that naturally provide more information into their decision-making process are two ways to improve interpretability.

CHAPTER 2

AI and ML in Healthcare

Learning Objective

This chapter explores the applications of AI in disease diagnosis, predictive analytics, personalised medicine, medical imaging, robotics, and drug discovery and development.

2.1 AI for Disease Diagnosis

Artificial Intelligence (AI) is transforming the healthcare landscape, and one of its most promising applications is in disease diagnosis. By leveraging advanced algorithms, machine learning, and data analytics, AI systems have the potential to revolutionise the way diseases are identified, enabling faster, more accurate, and cost-effective diagnostic processes.

1. Principles of AI in Disease Diagnosis

At its core, AI in disease diagnosis relies on the processing and analysis of large datasets, often referred to as big data. These datasets include medical records, imaging data, genetic information, and even patient-reported outcomes. By employing Machine Learning (ML) techniques, AI systems learn to identify patterns and correlations within the data that may not be apparent to human clinicians. Key technologies underpinning AI in this domain include:

a. **Machine Learning (ML):** ML algorithms are trained on large datasets to recognise patterns and make predictions. For instance, supervised learning models can be used to classify diseases based on labelled data, while unsupervised learning can identify clusters or anomalies in datasets.

b. **Deep Learning (DL):** A subset of ML, deep learning employs neural networks to process complex and high-dimensional data such as medical images. Convolutional Neural Networks (CNNs), for example, are widely used in image-based diagnostics.

c. **Natural Language Processing (NLP):** NLP techniques enable AI to analyse unstructured text data, such as clinical notes or medical literature, providing insights into patient conditions and aiding in diagnosis.

d. **Computer Vision:** This field focuses on enabling machines to interpret visual data, making it particularly valuable in radiology, pathology, and dermatology.

2. Applications of AI in Disease Diagnosis

AI has found applications in diagnosing a wide array of diseases across medical specialities. Some notable examples include:

a. **Radiology:** AI systems can analyse medical imaging data such as X-rays, CT scans, and MRIs to detect abnormalities like tumours, fractures, and pulmonary diseases. For instance, AI algorithms have been developed to identify early signs of lung cancer with remarkable accuracy.

b. **Pathology:** In pathology, AI-powered image analysis tools assist in detecting cancerous cells in histopathological slides, reducing diagnostic time and improving precision.

c. **Cardiology:** AI models are used to interpret electrocardiograms (ECGs) and echocardiograms, identifying conditions such as arrhythmias, heart failure, and congenital heart defects.

d. **Ophthalmology:** AI algorithms can diagnose eye diseases like diabetic retinopathy, glaucoma, and age-related macular degeneration by analysing retinal images.

e. **Infectious Diseases:** During the COVID-19 pandemic, AI tools were deployed to detect infection from chest imaging and to predict disease progression.

f. **Mental Health:** NLP-based AI tools analyse speech patterns and text inputs to screen for mental health conditions such as depression and anxiety.

g. **Primary Care:** AI-powered chatbots and virtual assistants aid in preliminary diagnosis by gathering symptoms and providing recommendations for further medical consultation.

3. Advantages of AI in Disease Diagnosis

The integration of AI into disease diagnosis offers several advantages:

a. **Increased Accuracy:** AI algorithms can analyse data with a level of precision that surpasses human capability, reducing misdiagnosis rates.

b. **Speed:** Automated analysis significantly shortens the time required for diagnostic procedures, enabling quicker treatment decisions.

c. **Cost-Effectiveness:** By automating routine diagnostic tasks, AI can lower healthcare costs, making quality care more accessible.

d. **Early Detection:** AI excels at identifying subtle patterns in data, facilitating the early detection of diseases when treatment is most effective.

e. **Scalability:** AI systems can handle large volumes of data, making them suitable for widespread screening programs.

f. **Personalisation:** By integrating data from various sources, AI can provide personalised diagnostic insights tailored to individual patient profiles.

2.2 Machine Learning in Predictive Analytics

Predictive analytics and machine learning are inextricably linked, as predictive models frequently incorporate a machine learning algorithm. These models can be trained to respond to new data or values over time, thereby delivering the results that businesses require.

These machine learning algorithms enable businesses to automate decision-making processes, make more precise predictions, scale up to manage large datasets and complex problems and acquire valuable insights to enhance their decision-making processes.

1. Using Machine Learning Models for Predictive Analytics

Machine Learning (ML) models are gaining popularity in predictive analytics due to their ability to provide more precise and accurate predictions than traditional statistical models. Depending on the specific issue that needs to be resolved, predictive analytics can be implemented using a variety of machine learning models.

Predictive analytics employs several prevalent machine learning models, including:

a) **Linear regression**: A continuous dependent variable is predicted using this model, which is based on one or more independent variables.

b) **Decision trees**: This paradigm employs a tree-like structure to depict decisions and their potential repercussions.

c) **Random Forest**: In order to enhance accuracy and prevent overfitting, this ensemble model integrates numerous decision trees. Overfitting in predictive analytics is the phenomenon of a model that is unable to generalise well to new data as a result of being trained too closely on its training data. This can result in subpar performance on unobserved data and inaccurate predictions.

d) **Support Vector Machines (SVM)**: This approach uses the best-separating hyperplane to categorise data into two or more groups. A linear decision boundary that separates two classes of data points is known as a separating hyperplane. It is a valuable instrument for classification tasks, including predicting the likelihood of a customer churning, determining whether a loan applicant is likely to default, and determining whether a medical image contains a tumour.

e) **Neural networks:** These models are designed to be applicable for both regression and classification, and they are motivated by the structure and functionality of the human brain.

2. Understanding Predictive Modelling Algorithms

Predictive modelling algorithms are a collection of statistical techniques and mathematical equations that are employed to forecast future behaviour or outcomes based on historical data. These algorithms are used to create predictive models that can recognise patterns in data, anticipate future trends, and make judgements based on facts. Finance, healthcare, marketing, and fraud detection are just a few of the many industries that use predictive modelling algorithms.

Several predictive modelling algorithms are well-known. These include:

a) Linear Regression

This algorithm is employed to forecast a continuous dependent variable using one or more independent variables. It assumes that the dependent and independent variables have a linear relationship (figure 2.1).

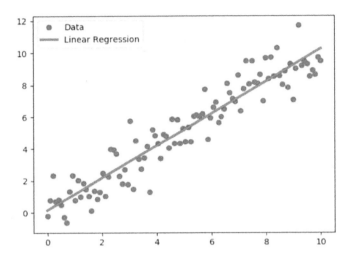

Figure 2.1: Linear Regression. [4]

b) Decision Trees

This algorithm employs a tree-like structure to depict decisions and their potential repercussions. It is a widely used algorithm for the solution of regression and classification problems. The decision tree can be

---

[4]https://res.cloudinary.com/talend/image/upload/w_1474/q_auto/qlik/glossary/predictive-analytics/seo-predictive-modeling-regression_ojr1jl.png

understood as the figure 2.2 given below.

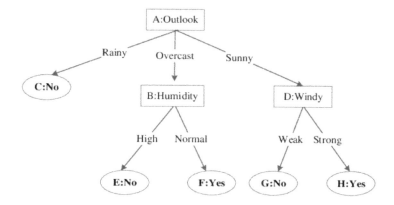

Figure 2.2: Decision Trees. [5]

c) Random Forest

The accuracy of this algorithm is enhanced and overfitting is prevented by combining multiple decision trees in an ensemble model.

d) Support Vector Machines (SVM)

This algorithm is employed to classify data into two or more categories by identifying the most effective separating hyperplane. It is a widely used algorithm for the classification of text and images.

e) Neural Networks

---

[5]https://res.cloudinary.com/talend/image/upload/w_1474/q_auto /qlik/glossary/predictive-analytics/seo-predictive-modeling-decision-tree_pfzfny.png

These algorithms can be employed for both classification and regression, and they are motivated by the structure and function of the human brain. They are composed of interconnected modules that process information and generate predictions.

f) K-Nearest Neighbours (KNN)

By identifying the k-nearest neighbours of a data point, this algorithm is employed for regression and classification. It is a widely used algorithm for the classification of images and text.

g) Naive Bayes

This algorithm is employed for classification and is predicated on Bayes' theorem. It determines each class's probability using the input characteristics and assumes that the features are independent of one another.

h) Gradient Boosting

This algorithm is an ensemble algorithm that enhances accuracy by combining multiple feeble learners. It is a widely used algorithm for the solution of classification and regression problems.

3. Benefits of Machine Learning in Predictive Analytics

"Improved accuracy, automated predictions, scalability, and better decision-making" are some of the main advantages of machine learning in predictive analytics. Machine learning algorithms can be used in predictive analytics to provide more precise and accurate predictions, automate decision-making processes, and scale up to manage large datasets and complex problems.

a) Improved Accuracy

More precise predictions can be made by machine learning algorithms than by conventional statistical models. Consequently, machine learning algorithms are capable of identifying patterns and relationships in data that may not be readily apparent to human analysts. The accuracy of machine learning algorithms can be enhanced over time by adapting to changing data patterns.

b) Automated Predictions

Decision-making processes can be automated and time can be saved through the use of machine learning algorithms. Machine learning algorithms are particularly advantageous in applications such as fraud detection, as they can rapidly analyse extensive datasets and automatically detect fraudulent transactions. By optimising inventory levels and delivery schedules, automated predictions can also be employed to expedite business processes, including supply chain management.

c) Scalability

Machine learning algorithms are capable of scaling up to address complex problems and large datasets.

This is especially advantageous in applications such as image classification or speech recognition, where the volume of data can be substantial.

In the context of sensor data from IoT devices, machine learning algorithms can also be employed to analyse data in real time. This enables businesses to promptly adjust to evolving circumstances and make data-driven decisions.

d) Improved Decision Making

Machine learning algorithms can offer insights that assist decision-makers in making more informed decisions. For instance, patterns in customer behaviour can be identified and targeted marketing campaigns can be developed using machine learning algorithms. By examining consumer demand and rival pricing, machine learning algorithms may also be used to optimise pricing strategies, including dynamic pricing. These insights have the potential to enhance the decision-making processes of organisations and provide them with a competitive advantage.

e) Flexibility

Semi-structured, unstructured, and structured data are just a few of the kinds of data that machine learning algorithms can manage. This enables businesses to acquire insights that were previously unavailable by analysing data from a variety of sources.

2.3   Personalised Medicine and Treatment Plans

Precision medicine, which is another name for personalised medicine, is the practice of making medical choices, actions, and treatments that are specific to each patient. Customised and targeted care is achieved by integrating patient data, such as "genetic information, biomarkers, clinical data, and lifestyle factors".

Healthcare professionals can enhance the precision of disease progression predictions, develop personalised treatment plans, and make more accurate diagnoses by comprehending the distinctive characteristics of each patient.

1. Implications for Treatment Personalisation

It is imperative to comprehend and account for the individual variability in patient responses to treatments to provide personalised healthcare.

Healthcare providers can enhance therapeutic outcomes, minimise adverse effects, and optimise treatment plans by taking these variations into account. The following are several significant implications:

a) Precision Medicine Approaches

Precision medicine, which is also referred to as personalised medicine, is designed to customise remedies according to the unique genetic profiles and characteristics of each patient.

Healthcare providers can determine the most effective treatment strategies for a specific patient by examining the genetic composition, biomarkers, and other pertinent data. By reducing the occurrence of trial and error, this method enhances the likelihood of effective results.

b) Pharmacogenomics Testing

Pharmacogenomics is the process of predicting an individual's response to medications by examining their genetic variations. Healthcare providers can ascertain the most appropriate medications and dosages for a patient by identifying specific genetic markers.

Pharmacogenomics testing is instrumental in the reduction of adverse drug reactions, the optimisation of treatment efficacy, and the enhancement of medication safety.

c) Therapeutic Drug Monitoring

Treatment efficacy and optimal dosing are guaranteed through therapeutic drug monitoring, which entails the measurement of drug levels in a patient's bloodstream. Through the tracking of medication concentrations over time, medical professionals may modify dosing schedules to accommodate individual differences in drug metabolism & clearance rates.

Maintaining drug levels within the therapeutic range is achieved through this method, which optimises treatment efficacy while minimising toxicity.

d) Patient Engagement and Shared Decision-Making

The recognition of individual variability fosters patient

engagement and collaborative decision-making. Healthcare providers can work with patients to create treatment programs that are tailored to their individual preferences, characteristics, and objectives.

Patient satisfaction rises, treatment adherence improves, and outcomes are enhanced when patients are allowed to actively engage in their healthcare choices.

e) Real-Time Monitoring and Feedback

Patient health metrics can be continuously monitored through real-time monitoring and feedback systems, including mobile health applications and peripheral devices. These technologies offer significant insights into the real-time responses of patients to treatments.

Healthcare providers can guarantee personalised care by promptly modifying treatment plans based on data on adherence to medication, vital signs, symptoms, and lifestyle factors.

2. The Rise of AI in Personalised Healthcare

Healthcare is not an exception to the revolution that AI has brought to various industries. AI algorithms can identify patterns, generate predictions, and offer healthcare professionals insights that were previously unavailable due to their capacity to analyse enormous quantities of intricate data.

AI is essential in the processing and interpretation of a

variety of datasets in personalised healthcare, which is used to produce actionable information that enhances patient care.

a) Data Integration and Analysis

AI's capacity to incorporate and analyse vast quantities of patient data is one of its most significant contributions to personalised healthcare. Data from electronic health records, genetic information, imaging, and wearable devices can be combined by AI algorithms to identify pertinent patterns and associations.

Healthcare providers can make more precise diagnoses and treatment decisions as a result of the exhaustive comprehension of each patient's health profile that this integrated analysis provides.

b) Predictive Analytics

Predictive analytics powered by AI are an additional indispensable element of personalised healthcare. AI algorithms can predict disease progression, identify risk factors, and estimate the response to specific treatments by utilising historical patient data.

By leveraging this predictive capability, healthcare providers can proactively manage diseases, customise treatments, and intervene earlier, resulting in improved patient outcomes.

c) Real-time Monitoring and Decision Support

Continuous feedback on patients' health status is made possible by AI technology, which enables real-time monitoring. The data collected by wearable devices that are endowed with sensors can include "vital signs, activity levels, sleep patterns, and other pertinent metrics."

Healthcare professionals may be informed of any departures from typical ranges or possible health hazards by using AI algorithms that can evaluate this data in real-time. Healthcare professionals are enabled to intervene promptly and deliver opportune interventions as a result of this real-time monitoring.

d) Image Recognition and Diagnosis

AI algorithms have exhibited exceptional capabilities in the areas of image recognition and diagnosis. Medical images, including X-rays, CT scans, and MRIs, can be analysed with exceptional precision by deep learning algorithms, a subset of AI.

AI algorithms can identify subtle abnormalities that may elude the human eye by comparing images with extensive databases of existing knowledge. This capability improves diagnostic accuracy, facilitates earlier disease detection, and facilitates more precise treatments.

3. Benefits of AI in Personalised Healthcare

The incorporation of AI in personalised healthcare offers numerous advantages to both patients and healthcare providers.

a) Improved Diagnostics

AI algorithms are capable of analysing intricate datasets and recognising patterns that may not be readily apparent to human observers. The risk of misdiagnosis is reduced, and early detection of maladies is facilitated by this advanced analytical capability, which enhances diagnostic accuracy.

Healthcare providers can enhance patient outcomes and provide more effective treatments by detecting diseases at an earlier stage.

b) Customised Treatment Plans

The objective of personalised healthcare is to offer treatment programs that are tailored to the individual requirements of each patient. In order to generate personalised treatment recommendations, AI algorithms evaluate individual attributes, including heredity, lifestyle factors, and biomarkers. These customised treatment plans provide patients with the highest quality of care by optimising therapeutic outcomes and minimising adverse effects.

c) Enhanced Patient Engagement

Patients can actively engage in their healthcare through the use of AI technology, including mobile applications and wearable devices. Patients may make well-informed lifestyle decisions and track their progress by receiving real-time data on vital signs, activity levels, and other health parameters. This heightened level of involvement encourages patients to assume a more proactive approach to the management of chronic conditions and the preservation of their health.

d) Streamlined Clinical Workflows

Healthcare providers can concentrate on patient care by automating routine administrative duties with the assistance of AI algorithms.

For instance, "Natural Language Processing (NLP)" algorithms can extract pertinent information from clinical notes, thereby eliminating the necessity for manual data entry. As a result of this automation, healthcare professionals can devote more time to patients and provide higher-quality care by alleviating the administrative burden.

e) Cost Savings

Healthcare systems have the potential to achieve cost reductions through personalised healthcare systems that are propelled by AI. Through the implementation of targeted treatments and early disease detection, AI has the potential to decrease the necessity for costly interventions and hospitalisations.

Additionally, AI algorithms can enhance operational efficiency, reduce superfluous procedures, and optimise resource allocation, resulting in substantial cost reductions for healthcare providers as well as payers.

2.4 AI in Medical Imaging and Robotics

Medical imaging in the context of artificial intelligence employs sophisticated algorithms to analyse medical images, enhance precision and efficiency in healthcare, and improve diagnostics.

1. AI and Deep Learning for Medical Image Analysis

Modern medical imaging is increasingly utilising Artificial Intelligence (AI) to enhance image interpretation and analysis. Artificial intelligence algorithms can be trained to analyse medical images and identify subtle changes or abnormalities that may be challenging for humans to identify. This can result in more precise and efficient diagnosis and treatment of a variety of conditions.

AI systems may identify lung nodules on CT scans, Alzheimer's disease symptoms on MRI scans, and early indicators of breast cancer on mammograms. AI can also be employed to analyse echocardiograms to diagnose cardiac disease and evaluate heart function.

Furthermore, artificial intelligence has the potential to enhance the precision and efficacy of radiology reports by autonomously producing preliminary data through the examination of medical imagery. This has the potential to enhance patient care by reducing the burden on radiologists and delivering more accurate and timely reports.

Consequently, it is imperative to guarantee that AI

algorithms are created and implemented in collaboration with human healthcare providers to deliver the highest quality of patient treatment.

2. The Role of AI in Improving Medical Imaging Diagnostics

AI is being utilised more and more to automate standard medical imaging operations including data administration, image processing, and quality control. AI can enhance the efficacy and accuracy of medical imaging, resulting in superior patient care, by outsourcing these tasks.

AI can autonomously segment and designate structures in medical images, including organs and tumours, thereby reducing the time and effort necessary for human healthcare providers. AI can also conduct quality control checks on medical images to guarantee that they satisfy the requisite standards for diagnosis and treatment.

Additionally, AI can be employed to manage and organise vast quantities of medical imaging data, thereby simplifying the process of accessing and analysing this data for healthcare providers. This can enhance the precision and efficacy of diagnosis and treatment by furnishing healthcare providers with a more thorough understanding of the patient's medical history and imaging data.

AI can assist healthcare providers in reducing their burden and enhancing the quality of patient care by automating routine duties in medical imaging. Nevertheless, it is imperative to guarantee that AI algorithms are developed and employed in a responsible and ethical manner, with a particular emphasis on patient safety and privacy.

3. From Image to Diagnosis: AI-Powered Medical Imaging Techniques

AI is increasingly being employed to aid in the prognosis and risk assessment of medical imaging as technology continues to advance.

Medical image analysis is one application in which AI is employed to predict the occurrence of specific conditions or identify potential health hazards. For instance, AI can be employed to analyse CT or MRI imaging to identify cancer signs or detect the early phases of Alzheimer's disease.

Risk assessment is an additional application of AI in medical imaging. Artificial intelligence (AI) algorithms may be trained on massive collections of medical pictures and related patient data to find risk factors that might result in specific medical disorders. Healthcare providers can subsequently employ this information to make more informed decisions regarding treatment options or to implement preventative measures to mitigate the likelihood of the development of specific conditions.

AI can analyse vast quantities of data with precision and speed, which is one of its advantages in the field of medical imaging.

Nevertheless, it is crucial to recognise that AI does not supplant healthcare providers. AI can aid in the analysis of medical images; however, the ultimate responsibility for the final diagnosis and treatment decisions is with the healthcare provider, who must consider all available information.

4. AI-Enabled Personalised Medicine: Revolutionising Patient Care

Personalised treatment planning entails the customisation of medical treatments to the specific needs of individual patients, taking into account their genetic composition, medical history, and lifestyle factors. AI is being utilised more frequently in personalised treatment planning to assist healthcare providers in making more informed decisions regarding treatment options.

Predictive modelling is one method by which AI is employed in personalised treatment planning. With the ability to analyse vast datasets of patient information, AI algorithms can predict the likelihood of a patient's response to various treatments and identify patterns.

Image analysis is another method by which AI is employed. For instance, AI algorithms can identify specific features that suggest a specific condition by analysing medical images, such as CT or MRI scans. This has the potential to augment the effectiveness of treatment outcomes by enabling healthcare providers to diagnose conditions more accurately and earlier.

To offer more personalised treatment recommendations, AI can be implemented in conjunction with "Electronic Health Records (EHRs)". An extensive amount of data on a patient's medical history, including previous diagnoses, treatments, and prescriptions, may be found in electronic health records. This information can be analysed by AI algorithms to identify potential hazards and prescribe Personalised treatment plans that are tailored to the patient's unique health profile.

All things considered, the use of AI in individualised treatment planning holds promise for bettering patient outcomes by customising medical interventions to meet the requirements of each patient. Nevertheless, it is crucial to emphasise that AI should not supplant healthcare providers; rather, it should be employed as an instrument to assist in their decision-making processes.

5. Advances in Medical Imaging through AI and Computer Vision

AI can assist researchers in the analysis of extensive medical image datasets, thereby identifying patterns or trends that may be challenging or impossible for humans to identify.

The development of novel imaging modalities is one area in which AI is being employed. For instance, researchers use AI to analyse data from various imaging modalities, including CT, MRI, and PET scans, to identify the strengths and limitations of each modality and to ascertain how they can be combined to enhance diagnostic accuracy.

AI is also being employed to enhance the precision of current imaging modalities. For instance, researchers are utilising AI to create algorithms that can automatically decrease noise and rectify picture distortion in medical imaging, improving the images' quality and accuracy.

Image analysis is another method by which AI is being employed in medical imaging research. Artificial intelligence algorithms can evaluate medical photos and pinpoint traits that could point to a certain illness or condition, like cancer. This has the potential to assist researchers in the development of more precise diagnostic instruments and the enhancement of treatment outcomes.

6. Artificial Intelligence and Robotics in Healthcare: The Emergence of Robot Doctors

At present, no robot doctor is capable of independently diagnosing patients. Although some robots, including surgical robots, are being created for use in healthcare, they are usually used in tandem with human healthcare professionals. They are incapable of autonomously diagnosing patients.

Nevertheless, AI has demonstrated potential in the diagnosis of specific conditions using medical imaging data and other patient information. More precise diagnoses and better patient outcomes might result from training AI systems to analyse medical pictures and identify anomalies or minute changes that would be hard for humans to notice.

It is crucial to recognise that AI algorithms are incapable of substituting human healthcare providers. Although they can offer valuable support and insights into the diagnosis and treatment of specific conditions, they lack the same level of clinical judgement and experience as human healthcare providers. Consequently, AI should be employed as an instrument to assist healthcare providers, rather than to supplant them.

2.5 Applications in Drug Discovery and Development

The process of drug discovery is a difficult and time-consuming endeavour. This process entails the identification of potential compounds, meticulous analysis, and rigorous testing to guarantee the safety and efficacy of new medications. Nevertheless, the field of drug discovery is enduring a remarkable transformation as a result of the accelerated advancement of technology. This revolution is being significantly influenced by machine learning, a potent instrument in the field of artificial intelligence.

This field has several critical applications of machine learning, including:

1. **Drug Target Identification:** Proteins or genes related to disease are examples of possible

therapeutic targets that may be found via machine learning analysis of biological data. Additionally, this assists researchers in concentrating their endeavours on the most prospective avenues.

2. **Drug Repurposing:** Through the analysis of existing data and the identification of potential candidates for repositioning, ML models can forecast the potential applications of existing pharmaceuticals in the treatment of new diseases.

3. **Chemoinformatic:** Based on chemical structures and properties, machine learning may help in the discovery of novel therapeutic molecules by forecasting their toxicity, activity, and other characteristics.

4. **Virtual Screening:** ML algorithms can be employed to virtually screen extensive chemical libraries to identify potential drug candidates, thereby reducing the number of compounds that must be synthesised and tested in the laboratory.

5. **Pharmacokinetics and Pharmacodynamics (PK/PD):** In order to optimise dosing and reduce adverse effects, ML models can predict the absorption, distribution, metabolism, and excretion of pharmaceuticals in the body, as well as their effects on the target.

6. **Drug-Drug Interaction Prediction:** Machine learning is essential for the prevention of adverse effects that may result from the concurrent use of multiple medications, as it assists in the

identification of potential interactions between various medicines.

7. **Clinical Trial Optimisation:** ML can assist in the recruitment and stratification of patients for clinical trials, thereby increasing the efficiency of the trials and reducing costs.

8. **Biomarker Discovery:** In the context of disease diagnosis, treatment response prediction, and patient outcome monitoring, machine learning has the potential to identify prospective biomarkers.

9. **Adverse Event Detection:** ML may be used to track real-world data, such as electronic health records, to identify and evaluate drug-related adverse events. Machine learning is the optimal choice due to the quantitative nature of data.

10. **Genomic Medicine:** Machine learning models can analyse genetic data to personalise treatment options, thereby matching medications to a patient's distinctive genetic profile.

11. **Drug Formulation and Delivery:** ML may help improve medicine formulations and delivery systems, increasing their efficacy and patient-friendliness.

12. **Drug Manufacturing:** The drug manufacturing process can be optimised through the use of machine learning, which can reduce production costs and ensure quality control.

13. **Drug Safety and Pharmacovigilance:** To monitor and guarantee the safety of medications on the

market, ML models can analyse data from a variety of sources, including the identification of adverse effects and the evaluation of long-term safety.

14. **Drug Pricing and Market Access:** Pricing strategies and the evaluation of the market access as well as the reimbursement environment for new medications may both benefit from machine learning.

15. **Drug Combination Therapy:** Machine learning can assist in the identification of effective drug combinations that produce synergistic effects in the treatment of complex diseases such as cancer.

CHAPTER 3

AI and ML in Business and Finance

Learning Objective

This chapter discusses the integration of AI in customer relationship management, fraud detection, algorithmic trading, business analytics, and risk assessment in the business and finance sectors.

3.1 AI in Customer Relationship Management

Artificial Intelligence (AI) has emerged as a game-changer in the constantly changing "landscape of business and Customer Relationship Management (CRM)". AI is transforming the manner in which companies engage with their consumers, resulting in interactions that are more personalised and efficient than ever. This transition is not merely a technological advancement; it is a strategic necessity for organisations that endeavour to remain competitive and relevant in the rapidly evolving and interconnected world of today.

1. The Power of AI in CRM

CRM has the potential to be transformed in numerous ways by artificial intelligence, which can analyse enormous quantities of data, identify patterns, and make real-time decisions.

a) Predictive Analytics

AI has made one of the most substantial contributions to CRM through predictive analytics. AI can anticipate future trends by examining historical data and customer behaviour, including the products or services that a customer is most likely to purchase and the time at which they are most likely to make a purchase. This enables businesses to customise their marketing and sales strategies to ensure that the appropriate message is conveyed at the appropriate time, thereby increasing the probability of a sale.

b) Personalisation

AI can analyse consumer data and preferences to generate exceedingly personalised experiences. This feature has the potential to enhance engagement and conversions by suggesting products, services, or content that are most pertinent to specific consumers. Customised offers, tailored recommendations, and personalised marketing messages not only improve the consumer experience but also help to cultivate customer loyalty.

c) Automation

Chatbots and virtual assistants that are fuelled by AI have become indispensable instruments in CRM. In addition to managing routine customer enquiries, these chatbots are capable of offering 24/7 support and even assisting with more intricate duties. In addition to decreasing response times, automation releases human agents to concentrate on interactions that are more complex and valuable.

d) Sentiment Analysis

To comprehend customer sentiment and feedback, AI can analyse text and social media data. Businesses can promptly identify and resolve issues and capitalise on positive feedback by monitoring consumer reviews and social media channels. This real-time feedback cycle enables organisations to make continuous improvements to their products and services.

e) Lead Scoring

Artificial intelligence-driven lead scoring assists sales teams in prioritising leads by evaluating their likelihood of conversion. AI is capable of generating a lead score by analysing a variety of factors, including demographics, behaviour, and engagement. This guarantees that sales teams concentrate their efforts on the most prospective leads. This not only enhances sales efficiency but also facilitates the more efficient closing of transactions.

f) Customer Churn Prediction

AI can identify which clients are most likely to churn—that is, go to a rival—by examining their feedback, using trends and behaviour. Businesses can mitigate revenue loss and minimise customer turnover by promptly identifying at-risk customers and implementing proactive retention strategies.

2. Implementing AI in CRM

The integration of AI into CRM necessitates meticulous planning and execution. Businesses should take into account the following steps:

a) Data Quality and Integration

AI is reliant on data. Clean, high-quality data is necessary to enable AI to function effectively in CRM. Establish data governance to guarantee data accuracy and consistency, in addition to data integration across all pertinent systems and platforms.

b) Choose the Right AI Tools

Each AI tool and platform has its own strengths and limitations, and there are numerous options available in the market. Businesses should conduct a thorough assessment of their requirements and select AI solutions that are most compatible with their CRM objectives.

c) Training and Expertise

Expertise is necessary for the implementation of AI. To guarantee that their teams can derive valuable insights from AI tools and utilise them effectively, businesses should allocate resources to training and development.

d) Continuous Monitoring and Optimisation

AI technology is not a "set it and forget it" proposition. It necessitates continuous optimisation and monitoring to guarantee that it is producing the desired outcomes. Businesses should conduct routine evaluations of AI performance and implement modifications as necessary.

e) Customer Privacy and Data Security

Businesses are obligated to prioritise data privacy and security as AI systems acquire and analyse customer data. It is imperative to adhere to data protection regulations and conduct ethical data management to preserve consumer trust.

3.2   Machine Learning in Fraud Detection

There is a growing use of machine learning in fraud detection across e-commerce businesses, governments, applications, and online services to identify and thwart sophisticated, frequently automated attacks that pose risks to infrastructure and aim to steal data, goods, and funds.

To detect fraud, it is essential for machine learning models to be trained on historical data related to fraudulent activities, including attack attempts, sources, and methods. Machine learning algorithms are capable of identifying patterns within historical datasets and subsequently adjusting a solution's security protocols to thwart future fraudulent activities, including those employing previously unseen techniques.

Machine learning serves as the most effective solution to the changing landscape of online threats, providing users with a significant edge in combating card fraud, the creation of fake accounts, account takeovers (ATOs), and credential stuffing.

1. Major Benefits of Machine Learning for Fraud Detection

Employing machine learning models for fraud detection, rather than relying on manual supervision, presents a significant advantage for businesses due to several benefits:

a) **Cost-Effectiveness:** Automating fraud detection and utilising machine learning leads to a reduction in costs related to manual fraud detection, encompassing expenses for labour, technology, and time. This enables the allocation of resources more efficiently and leads to a reduction in overall expenses related to combating fraud.

b) **Accuracy:** The purpose of training machine learning algorithms on large data sets is to detect patterns and anomalies that are impossible for humans to detect (and at a pace that is beyond their capabilities). Monitored ML can greatly decrease the occurrence of false positives and false negatives, which are essential indicators of detection accuracy when compared to conventional manual methods.

c) **Relentlessness:** Humans are capable of analysing data for only a limited number of hours each day, whereas machines can operate continuously, without experiencing burnout or overload. The performance of an ML algorithm typically improves with the increase in the volume of data processed.

2. Applications of Machine Learning in Fraud Detection

Machine learning is increasingly being employed in the prevention and detection of fraud as a result of its capacity to analyse vast quantities of data, recognise patterns, and adjust to new information. Several prevalent applications of machine learning in the prevention of fraud are as follows:

a) **Anomaly detection**: Transactional data can be analysed using machine learning algorithms to detect anomalies or deviations from the norm. Through "training" on past data, the algorithms can identify valid transactions and identify questionable activity that could point to fraud.

b) **Risk scoring**: Risk scores can be assigned to transactions or user accounts by machine learning models based on a variety of factors, including "transaction amount, location, frequency, and prior behaviour". Organisations can prioritise their resources and concentrate on specific transactions or accounts that require further investigation by determining that higher risk scores indicate a greater likelihood of fraud.

c) **Network analysis**: In order to execute their activities, fraudulent actors frequently establish networks and collaborate. Through the investigation of interconnections between items (such as people, accounts, or devices) and the discovery of odd connections or clusters, machine learning methods like graph analysis may assist in revealing these networks.

d) **Text analysis**: The identification of patterns or keywords that may suggest fraud or schemes is possible through the analysis of unstructured text data, including emails, social media posts, and customer reviews, by machine learning algorithms.

e) **Identity verification**: To make sure someone is who they say they are and stop identity theft, machine learning models may examine and validate user-provided data, such as pictures of identification papers or facial recognition information.

f) **Adaptive learning**: The ability to learn and adjust to new information is one of the primary strengths of machine learning. It is possible to retrain machine learning models on new data as fraudulent actors alter their strategies, thereby enabling them to remain current and more capable of identifying emergent fraud patterns.

The utilisation of machine learning in fraud prevention can be a potent method for organisations to improve the overall security and consumer experience, reduce the risk of false positives, and enhance their detection capabilities.

3.3 Algorithmic Trading and Investment Strategies

Algorithmic trading, which is also known as automated trading, black-box trading, or algo-trading, is the process of placing a transaction using a computer program that adheres to a predetermined set of instructions (an algorithm). In theory, the transaction has the potential to produce profits at a rate and frequency that are unattainable for a human trader.

The specified sets of instructions are predicated on any mathematical model, price, quantity, or timing. In addition to providing the trader with profit opportunities, algorithmic trading enhances the liquidity of markets and the systematicity of trading by eliminating the influence of human emotions on trading activities.

1. Algorithmic Trading Strategies

In order to be profitable in terms of increased earnings or cost reduction, any algorithmic trading strategy must be based on an identified opportunity. The following are frequently employed trading strategies in algo-trading:

a) Trend-Following Strategies

The most prevalent algorithmic trading strategies are based on trends in price level movements, channel breakouts, moving averages, and related technical indicators. Through algorithmic trading, these strategies are the most straightforward and straightforward to

78

execute, as they do not necessitate any price forecasts or predictions. Without delving into the complexities of predictive analysis, trades are started in response to the emergence of favourable patterns, which are simple and quick to apply using algorithms. It is a prevalent trend-following strategy to employ 50- and 200-day moving averages.

b) Arbitrage Opportunities

The price differential is a risk-free profit or arbitrage that is achieved by purchasing a dual-listed stock at a reduced price in one market and selling it at a higher price in another market. The identical procedure can be applied to equities and futures instruments, as price differentials do occasionally exist. The efficient placement of orders and the identification of such price differentials through the implementation of an algorithm are profitable opportunities.

c) Index Fund Rebalancing

In order to align their holdings with their respective benchmark indices, index funds have established rebalancing periods. Depending on the number of stocks in the index fund just before index fund rebalancing, this generates attractive chances for algorithmic traders, who take advantage of projected transactions that give rewards ranging from 20 to 80 basis points. Algorithmic trading systems are employed to execute these transactions in a timely manner and at the most advantageous pricing.

d) Mathematical Model-Based Strategies

It is possible to trade on both the underlying securities and options using well-established mathematical models, such as the delta-neutral trading technique. Delta neutral is a portfolio strategy that consists of multiple positions with offsetting positive and negative deltas. This ratio compares the change in the price of an asset, typically a marketable security, to the corresponding change in the price of its derivative, ensuring that the overall delta of the assets in question is zero.

e) Trading Range (Mean Reversion)

The foundation of the mean reversion approach is the idea that an asset's high and low values are transient phenomena that eventually return to their mean value or average value. A price range can be identified and defined, and an algorithm can be implemented to autonomously execute transactions when the price of an asset varies within or outside of its defined range.

f) Volume-Weighted Average Price (VWAP)

The "Volume-Weighted Average Price" strategy dynamically determines smaller increments of a large order and releases them to the market by utilising stock-specific historical volume profiles. The objective is to implement the order close to the VWAP).

g) Time Weighted Average Price (TWAP)

The "Time-weighted average price" strategy divides a large order into smaller, dynamically determined portions that are released to the market in evenly spaced time intervals between a start and end time. The objective is to minimise the market impact by executing the order at a price that is close to the average between the start and end periods.

h) Percentage of Volume (POV)

This algorithm continues to send partial orders in accordance with the defined participation ratio and the volume traded in the markets until the trade order is fully filled. In the associated "steps strategy," orders are sent at a user-specified percentage of market volumes, and when the stock price hits user-specified thresholds, this participation rate is increased or decreased.

i) Implementation Shortfall

The "implementation shortfall" strategy is designed to reduce the execution cost of an order by trading off the real-time market. This approach saves on the order's cost and capitalises on the opportunity cost of delayed execution. When the stock price experiences a positive movement, the strategy will elevate the targeted participation rate, while it will decrease it when the stock price experiences a negative movement.

2. Advantages and Disadvantages of Algorithmic Trading

The following benefits are offered by algorithmic trading:

a. **Best Execution:** Trades are executed at the most favourable prices.

b. **Low Latency:** Trade orders are placed with precision and speed, ensuring a high likelihood of execution at the desired levels while mitigating significant price fluctuations.

c. **Reduced Transaction Costs:** Trading expenses are minimised.

d. **Simultaneous Market Analysis:** Automated systems assess multiple market conditions concurrently.

e. **Elimination of Human Error:** Manual errors and emotional or psychological biases in trading decisions are minimised.

f. **Backtesting:** Algorithms can be tested using historical and real-time data to determine their effectiveness as trading strategies.

Algorithmic trading also has numerous drawbacks or disadvantages to take into account:

a. **Latency:** Algorithmic trading is contingent upon the implementation of trades with rapidity and minimal latency, which comprises the delay in their execution. If a trade is not executed promptly, it may lead to lost opportunities or losses.

b. **Black Swan Events:** Algorithmic trading forecasts future market movements by employing mathematical models and historical data. Nevertheless, algorithmic traders may incur losses as a consequence of unforeseen market disruptions, which are referred to as "black swan events."

c. **Dependence on Technology:** Algorithmic trading is dependent on technology, which includes high-speed internet connections and computer programs. If technical difficulties or malfunctions occur, the trading process may be disrupted, leading to subsequent losses.

d. **Market Impact:** The market prices can be significantly influenced by large algorithmic trades, which can lead to losses for traders who are unable to modify their trades in response to these changes. In some instances, algorithmic trading has been suspected of contributing to market volatility, even resulting in "flash crashes."

e. **Regulation:** Compliance with the numerous regulatory requirements and oversight that algorithmic trading is subject to can be a time-consuming and intricate process.

f. **High Capital Costs:** Algorithmic trading system development and installation may be expensive, and traders may have to pay recurring fees for data feeds and software.

g. **Limited Customisation:** The capacity of traders to personalise their transactions to accommodate their unique requirements or preferences may be restricted by the pre-established rules and instructions of algorithmic trading systems.

h. **Lack of Human Judgment:** Due to its reliance on mathematical models and historical data, algorithmic trading ignores the subjective and qualitative elements that might affect market movements. For traders who favour a more intuitive or instinctive trading approach, this absence of human judgment can be a disadvantage.

3.4 AI-Powered Business Analytics

Business Analytics (BA) is the process of assessing data to assess business performance and derive insights that may aid in strategic planning. The objective is to determine the elements that have a direct effect on business performance, including "revenue, user engagement, and technical availability."

Data is gathered from various business levels, encompassing product, marketing, operations, and finance. At the IT layer, analytics exhibits a more direct causal relationship, whereas at the business layer, metrics are interdependent and their behaviour frequently fluctuates, resulting in a particularly complex process for business analytics.

1. AI in Business Analytics

Recently, agile and interactive dashboards have become the ideal solution for business analysts. For growing enterprises, the need for data analysis is surpassing what dashboards for "Key Performance Indicators (KPIs)) can provide.

The data analyst must manually identify relationships between KPIs across data silos to investigate the cause of a specific anomaly. Identifying the root cause of an underlying issue can require a considerable amount of time as analysts navigate through dashboards while employing a process of elimination.

Employing AI in business analytics enables organisations to leverage machine learning algorithms for identifying trends and extracting insights from intricate data sets sourced from various origins. Analytics powered by AI delves further into data and identifies simultaneous anomalies, uncovering essential insights into business operations.

AI-driven business analytics can independently learn and adjust to evolving behavioural patterns of metrics, making it considerably more accurate in identifying anomalies and deviations. This indicates a notable decrease in false positives and irrelevant alert storms, leading to the emergence of only the most critical business incidents.

In contrast to conventional BI tools, AI business analytics enables the detection of business incidents in real-time and the identification of root causes, allowing for quicker problem resolution and earlier opportunity capture.

2. Ways to Use AI Analytics

Analytics powered by AI can carry out tasks that are descriptive, predictive, and prescriptive. There are various uses and applications across the business and its systems. Four methods exist for utilising AI analytics. This includes:

a) Forecast Demand

As AI analytics possesses prognostic capabilities, it is capable of predicting product demand. "Available stock data, seasonal trends, and historical purchasing data" can be utilised by AI analytics to forecast future product demand for a business. This enables the enhancement of product stocking and the procurement of inventory or materials.

b) Unify Data

The rapid pace and extensive reach of AI analytics allow for the integration of data from multiple platforms and systems, resulting in a cohesive and comprehensive perspective. This proves to be particularly beneficial for those with diverse systems or for those looking to examine customer data across multiple platforms.

c) Predict Business Outcomes

AI analytics can process extensive data sets and, based on this analysis, can forecast effective outcomes or potential future events. This has the potential to enhance decision-making within a business, as it allows for visibility into the results of suggested actions.

d) Gain Audience Demographic insights

Valuable insights into the demographics of an audience can be offered through AI analytics. This encompasses buying behaviours, geographical location, age, and gender.

Gaining a deeper and more detailed understanding of the audience enables the personalisation of content and the optimisation of customer targeting.

3. Pros and Cons of AI-Powered Business Analytics

The implementation of AI analytics offers numerous benefits. The capability to broaden the scope of analytics can provide benefits to businesses in multiple ways:

a) **Greater Productivity:** AI analytics liberates individuals from the tedious and time-intensive responsibility of conducting data analysis independently. Time can be redirected towards more high-priority tasks. The rapid pace and extensive reach of AI analytics allow for the acquisition of quality insights almost instantly, enabling quicker actions and positive changes.

b) **Pattern Recognition:** AI analytics can identify and retrieve valuable insights from extensive datasets, even when they span various platforms. Machine learning can utilise this to identify trends and patterns. The integration of AI and ML has the potential to enhance business insights and predictions.

c) **Flexibility:** Machine learning algorithms enable AI analytics to continuously learn and adjust. AI analytics can be utilised for various enquiries and data sources, requiring only the input of information.

AI analytics has the potential to provide advantages for businesses, though it might not suit every organisation. It can be:

a) **Expensive:** The implementation of AI analytics demands significant investment in both time and resources. Implementing AI analytics may also require upgrading existing systems to fulfil the necessary requirements. Although the advantages of AI analytics for businesses will eventually offset the expense, this can lead to a significant bill that may not be a feasible investment at the moment for certain companies.

b) **Prone to Error:** AI analytics lessens the likelihood of human error; however, this does not eliminate the risk of errors entirely. AI analytics still require human interaction, and there is potential for user errors to occur. Design errors may arise from the training data that is used, including biased, tainted, insufficient, or incorrect data.

c) **Lack of Regulation:** Regulations concerning AI are gradually being implemented globally. Numerous industries continue to experience a deficiency in regulations. Companies must stay current with regulations and ensure their AI analytics systems align with the changing regulatory framework in their industry. Establishing risk frameworks is crucial for the effective management of AI analytics risks.

3.5   Machine Learning for Risk Assessment

Conducting an assessment for a risk analyst necessitates a significant amount of time and effort. In order to assess the potential hazards that a potential client may face, the process entails intensive research and analysis of a variety of factors. Additionally, due to the subjective nature of this process, it is not uncommon for a variety of risk analysts to provide alternative analyses of the same policy.

Nevertheless, machine learning can assist in the evolution of the risk assessment process by generating risk models that analyse the information recorded about previous policies to learn from their errors and successes. This process enables the evaluation of newly signed policies to be conducted more swiftly and reliably.

The prospective advantages of machine learning have led to its increasing adoption in the field of risk assessment. Businesses worldwide are emphasising the following prevalent use cases:

1.   Credit Risk Modelling

Credit risk modelling is the process of predicting the likelihood that a borrower would miss payments on a loan or otherwise fail to meet their financial commitments utilising methods and resources. To make more informed lending decisions, businesses, particularly financial institutions, will analyse a multitude of data, including a borrower's income, debt levels, and credit history. This assists them in reducing potential losses and monitoring their overall risk exposure.

Machine learning has revolutionised credit risk modelling in numerous ways by leveraging its predictive capabilities and sophisticated analytical techniques. At first, its algorithms are capable of analysing a diverse array of data to identify high-risk borrowers and identify potential default incidents before their occurrence. Secondly, they can autonomously evaluate the creditworthiness of a customer or entity to expedite the credit approval process and enhance credit scoring.

Lastly, machine learning can categorise consumers into distinct categories based on their credit behaviours and risk profiles. Even more, it can dynamically adjust credit limits or interest rates in response to real-time market conditions and data regarding a borrower's credit risk. This enables financial institutions to customise their loan terms, communication strategies, and offerings to ensure that they meet the requirements of their customers and that they are contented.

2. Detection of Credit Card Fraud & Money Laundering

Currently, a variety of financial institutions have implemented ML-based monitoring systems (also known as "workflow engines") in their credit card payment infrastructure. These systems are capable of identifying and blocking potentially peculiar transactions in real-time by scanning tremendous amounts of historical payment data.

Machine learning also substantially impedes money laundering activity. It is capable of swiftly combining transaction information from various sources and identifying intricate patterns in the data.

This provides organisations with a comprehensive understanding of a customer's activity, enables the identification of the probability of fraud, and significantly reduces the number of false positives.

Nevertheless, the detection of money laundering is a challenging task. Financial institutions frequently receive little feedback from law enforcement regarding which cases are classified as money laundering, as there is no universally accepted definition of the term. This implies that they rarely train machine learning models on these cases to identify money laundering activity.

Consequently, a significant number of institutions will rely on lower-level anomalous activity reports to enhance their ML risk management models. These reports categorise alerts as either legitimate cases (which appear to be potential fraud) or false alarms (which do not indicate actual money laundering).

Additionally, institutions employ unsupervised learning to identify potential hazards in the absence of pre-existing labels. In addition, they employ clustering to identify outliers and group similar data points, thereby identifying anomalies in the data.

3. Surveillance of Conduct Behaviours

Machine learning is now employed by companies to monitor and comprehend even the most intricate patterns in employee actions, as it is essential for maintaining ethical and compliant business practices.

For instance, machine learning will evaluate a trader's whole trading portfolio and individual deals in financial institutions. If ML identifies any indication of malfeasance, such as the opening of unauthorised cards or the violation of company policies, it will notify management or compliance teams to conduct a more thorough investigation. This mitigates the issue from worsening.

Machine learning can identify actions that deviate from these normal patterns and label them as dubious by learning from past activities that are considered "normal" behaviour.

Machine learning models can continually acquire new knowledge by utilising their past observations or actions, which they can then apply to alter their future behaviour over time. This procedure is frequently referred to as a "feedback loop." Therefore, machine learning models are capable of adjusting to any changes in employee behaviour and identifying future actions with greater precision.

4. Cybersecurity

In the current era, where hazards are constantly evolving, machine learning is essential for the analysis and management of cybercrime. Its algorithms are programmed to identify "typical" network activity. So, they will notify cybersecurity teams if they observe any suspicious indicators, such as an unexpected logon from a new location or unusual links within an email.

ML can analyse threat data from a variety of sources, such as phishing campaigns or malware databases, to identify established attack patterns and anticipate similar threats in the future. Certain machine learning models can autonomously mitigate threats by isolating affected systems, restricting access, or barring suspicious IP addresses. Additionally, ML surpasses conventional methodologies in its capacity to learn from historical events and consistently adjust to new, evolving threats.

5. Operations

Operational risk management is facilitated by machine learning, which autonomously identifies, evaluates, and mitigates risks associated with human activities and business processes. In particular, machine learning algorithms can analyse sensor data (e.g., temperature or vibration) from machinery to anticipate malfunctions before they occur. Consequently, this reduces maintenance expenses and delays.

ML also assists in the prevention of supply chain risks by analysing data from suppliers, market trends, and geopolitical events to predict potential disruptions. This enables companies to proactively adjust their operations, thereby preventing stock shortages or production delays. ML models can identify deviations from "normal" business processes, which can help to identify issues early on and prevent operational inefficiencies.

CHAPTER 4

AI and ML in Autonomous Systems

Learning Objective

This chapter covers the application of AI in autonomous vehicles, robotics, drones, intelligent traffic management systems, and smart cities, focusing on navigation, automation, and system efficiencies.

4.1 Autonomous Vehicles and AI Navigation

Autonomous Vehicles (AVs) represent a revolutionary leap in transportation technology, combining advanced sensors, Artificial Intelligence (AI), and Machine Learning (ML) to navigate roads with minimal or no human intervention. These self-driving vehicles promise to transform urban mobility, reduce accidents, and enhance traffic efficiency. At the heart of this innovation lies AI navigation—a sophisticated system of algorithms and data processing techniques that enable vehicles to perceive, interpret, and respond to their surroundings.

1. Core Technologies of Autonomous Vehicles

The development of autonomous vehicles is driven by the integration of several core technologies. These include:

a. **Sensors and Perception**: Autonomous vehicles rely on a variety of sensors to detect and understand their environment. These include:

    i. **LiDAR (Light Detection and Ranging):** LiDAR systems generate precise 3D maps of the vehicle's surroundings by emitting laser pulses and measuring their reflections.

    ii. **Cameras:** Cameras capture visual data, such as road signs, lane markings, and obstacles.

    iii. **Radar:** Radar sensors measure the distance and speed of objects, especially useful in adverse weather conditions.

    iv. **Ultrasonic Sensors:** These detect nearby objects, aiding in parking and low-speed manoeuvres.

b. **Connectivity**: Vehicle-to-Everything (V2X) communication allows AVs to interact with other vehicles, infrastructure, and pedestrians. This connectivity ensures real-time updates on traffic conditions, road hazards, and navigation routes.

c. **AI and Machine Learning**: AI is central to processing the vast amount of data collected by sensors. Machine learning algorithms help AVs recognize patterns, predict behaviours, and make decisions. Neural networks are particularly effective in tasks like image recognition and natural language processing, enabling the vehicle to comprehend its environment.

d. **High-Definition Mapping**: Accurate and detailed maps are crucial for AV navigation. These maps provide information about road geometry, traffic signals, and landmarks, complementing real-time sensor data.

2. The Role of AI in Navigation

AI navigation in autonomous vehicles encompasses several critical functions:

a. **Perception**: Perception systems allow the vehicle to identify objects, such as pedestrians, cyclists, and other vehicles. Using AI, the vehicle can classify these objects and assess their trajectories to avoid collisions.

b. **Localisation**: Localisation determines the vehicle's position within its environment. AI algorithms integrate data from GPS, Inertial Measurement Units (IMUs), and visual landmarks to achieve centimetre-level accuracy.

c. **Path Planning**: Path planning involves charting a safe and efficient route from the vehicle's current location to its destination. AI considers factors such as traffic, road conditions, and pedestrian activity to optimise the route.

d. **Control**: Control systems manage the vehicle's acceleration, braking, and steering. AI ensures smooth and responsive manoeuvres, maintaining safety and passenger comfort.

3. Levels of Autonomy

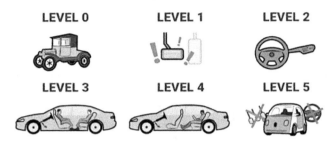

Figure 4.1: Automation Levels of Autonomous Cars. [6]

Autonomous vehicles are classified into six levels of autonomy (figure 4.1), as defined by the Society of Automotive Engineers (SAE):

a. **Level 0:** No automation. The driver controls all aspects of driving.

b. **Level 1:** Driver assistance. Systems like adaptive cruise control provide limited assistance.

c. **Level 2:** Partial automation. The vehicle can control steering and acceleration, but the driver must remain engaged.

---

[6]https://lh4.googleusercontent.com/69q_HJ3nPQGSSyrGqFbW4 QkQVd-9M6Kjh0iMXYydACQCXBj9tewW2vf7bg-Y2ZV7UldpkxhjnVnmbLB6NhXlZ09ZFgTFNf7151nBzKYGTYH YTuRVr-wWhGGqYP4ME3pBxxJfC50GuIETFCuwMf9Tf_WNdsxdkljB40 euG7EpH3kA388GijYVJTbzBQ

d. **Level 3:** Conditional automation. The vehicle can handle most tasks, but the driver must intervene when requested.

e. **Level 4:** High automation. The vehicle can operate autonomously in specific conditions without driver input.

f. **Level 5:** Full automation. The vehicle requires no human intervention under any conditions.

4. **Applications of Autonomous Vehicles**

Autonomous vehicles have a wide range of applications, including:

a. **Passenger Transportation**: Ride-hailing services and personal vehicles equipped with self-driving technology aim to provide safer and more efficient travel.

b. **Logistics and Delivery**: Autonomous trucks and drones are revolutionising logistics by enabling 24/7 operations and reducing delivery times.

c. **Public Transit**: Self-driving buses and shuttles can improve the accessibility and efficiency of public transportation systems.

d. **Agriculture and Mining**: Autonomous machinery in agriculture and mining increases productivity and safety in challenging environments.

4.2 AI in Robotics and Automation

Automation has become an integral part of modern

industries, revolutionising the way businesses operate and increasing productivity and efficiency.

Two major driving forces behind this transformation are Artificial Intelligence (AI) and Robotics. These technologies have evolved significantly in recent years, leading to groundbreaking advancements in robotics and automation across various sectors.

1.   The Role of AI in Robotics

The process of comprehending robotics and AI might be difficult and complex, but it can also be a thrilling chance to investigate advanced technology. The fields of robotics and artificial intelligence are developing quickly, with new developments occurring daily as these technologies offer a glimpse into the future of automation and human-computer interaction.

Understanding robotics and AI may be challenging and complex, but it can also be an exciting opportunity to research innovative technology. Robotics and artificial intelligence are sectors that are growing swiftly, with new advancements in robotics and automation happening every day as these technologies provide a glimpse into automation and human-computer interaction in the future.

2.   Need for AI and Robot Technologies

We need AI and robotics for their transformative potential in enhancing efficiency, precision, and productivity across various industries. These technologies can tackle repetitive tasks, work in hazardous environments, and handle complex data analysis, reducing human errors and risks. AI and robotics have the potential to address labour shortages in certain sectors and unlock new possibilities in healthcare, manufacturing, logistics, and more. Ultimately, their integration into automation leads to improved quality of life, increased innovation, and economic growth.

3. The Recent AI Advancements in robotics and automation

Robotics and AI developments have the potential to modernize several industries by improving productivity, lowering errors, and streamlining processes. They also bring up significant ethical and societal issues, such as the effect on employment and the requirement for strong laws and safety precautions as automation grows more pervasive. Here are some notable advancements in robotics and automation:

a) Deep Learning and Neural Networks

Deep learning techniques, such as Convolutional Neural Networks (CNNs) and Recurrent Neural Networks (RNNs), have improved automation by enabling machines to process and understand vast amounts of data. This has applications in image and speech recognition, as well as natural language processing.

b) Computer Vision

Computer vision algorithms have become more accurate

and efficient, enabling robots to perceive and interact with their environment more effectively. This is crucial in industries like manufacturing, where robots can identify and manipulate objects with precision.

c) Natural Language Processing (NLP)

Advances in NLP have led to improved human-robot interactions. Chatbots and virtual assistants are now capable of understanding and responding to natural language queries, making customer support and information retrieval more efficient.

d) Reinforcement Learning

Reinforcement learning has allowed robots to learn tasks through trial and error. Robots can now autonomously adapt to new environments and optimise their actions, making them more versatile in complex settings like logistics and autonomous vehicles.

e) Robotics Process Automation (RPA)

RPA is being increasingly used to automate repetitive, rule-based tasks in business processes. Bots can perform data entry, data extraction, and other routine tasks, freeing up human workers for more creative and strategic work.

f) Autonomous Vehicles

The development of self-driving cars and trucks is a prominent example of AI and robotics in automation. These vehicles use advanced sensors, machine learning algorithms, and real-time data to navigate and make driving safer and more efficient.

g) Industry 4.0 and Smart Manufacturing

AI-powered robots and automation systems are integral to the concept of Industry 4.0. Smart factories use IoT sensors, AI analytics, and robotics to optimise manufacturing processes, reduce downtime, and improve quality control.

h) Healthcare Robotics

Robots are increasingly assisting in healthcare settings, from robotic surgical systems to autonomous patient care robots. These systems improve precision and efficiency in medical procedures and patient care.

i) Agricultural Automation

AI-driven robots and drones are being used in agriculture for tasks like planting, harvesting, and monitoring crops. This helps optimise resource use and increase crop yields.

j) Warehouse and Logistics Automation

E-commerce companies and logistics providers are using robots and AI for warehouse automation. This includes autonomous drones and robots that pick, pack, and ship products, making supply chains more efficient.

4.3 Machine Learning in Drones and Unmanned Systems

Artificial intelligence has revolutionised the field of

Unmanned Aerial Vehicles (UAVs), which are more commonly referred to as drones. The primary application of drones was aerial photography or as a leisure. Initially, they were straightforward remotely piloted machines. Nevertheless, the autonomous execution of intricate tasks by drones has been significantly enhanced by the development of AI and machine learning, thereby representing a significant advancement in drone technology.

1. The Rise of AI/ML Drone Technology: How Drones Work with AI

Currently, drones are powered by a combination of technologies, including electronics, aerodynamics, artificial intelligence (AI) and computer vision. AI/ML has revolutionised drone technology. AI-equipped drones employ machine learning algorithms to collect and interpret data, thereby enabling them to make informed decisions during flight. In search and rescue missions and military drones, where prompt, real-time responses are essential, this autonomous capability is particularly apparent.

Drones that are propelled by AI are capable of operating in intricate environments, as evidenced by their use in military defence. The autonomous reconnaissance and surveillance capabilities of these unmanned drones are frequently facilitated by the inclusion of AI algorithms and sensors. Drones employ AI in search and rescue missions to find those in need, often in difficult-to-reach places. These drones' AI capabilities are enabled by edge computing, which processes the data and images acquired in real-time, facilitating rapid and effective rescue efforts.

In addition, the incorporation of AI has enabled the development of swarm technology, which mimics the collaborative behaviour of a swarm by allowing multiple drones to operate in a coordinated manner. This is achieved by the creation of AI algorithms that facilitate the communication and collective decision-making of drones. In addition, drone operation has been improved in sectors such as agricultural monitoring, where drones that are outfitted with AI can survey fields to monitor crop health and growth, providing producers with valuable data.

2. AI/ML in Drones: Transforming Autonomous Capabilities

Drones have been transformed by the incorporation of AI into their operations, which has allowed them to execute tasks with unparalleled precision and efficiency. Due to their improved capabilities in autonomous operation, object detection, and data analysis, AI-powered drones are becoming indispensable instruments in a variety of industries.

The primary application of Artificial Intelligence (AI) and Machine Learning (ML) in drones lies in computer vision, a branch of AI that allows drones to interpret visual data from their surroundings. Advanced AI algorithms, particularly neural networks, empower drones to detect and recognise objects, patterns, and anomalies. This capability enables drones to autonomously navigate complex environments, avoid obstacles, and make real-time decisions. Such functionalities are crucial in scenarios like search and rescue operations or monitoring and surveying inaccessible areas.

Artificial intelligence-equipped drones are capable of rapidly collecting and analysing vast quantities of data, a capability that is indispensable in applications such as infrastructure inspection, environmental surveillance, and agricultural monitoring for improving crop health. The efficient operation of drones in a variety of drone applications has been improved by the ability of drones to adjust their operation based on the data they acquire, thanks to the advancements in AI and machine learning models.

Furthermore, drones have been implemented in the context of emergency response and public protection. AI-powered drones can scan for missing persons, locate locations to support firefighting efforts and provide real-time aerial views to aid in disaster management. These unmanned aerial vehicles, which operate autonomously, serve as an illustration of the substantial effects and enhancements that the integration of drone technology and artificial intelligence can have on real-world situations.

3. Military Applications: AI/ML-Powered Drones in

Military Defense

The role of AI-powered drones in the realm of military defence has become increasingly significant. Utilising artificial intelligence in drones has revolutionised military operations, enabling more strategic and advanced applications. Military drones, which are frequently autonomous or referred to as "killer robots" by some, are essential in combat, surveillance, and reconnaissance scenarios.

One of the primary benefits of AI/ML in military drones is their capacity to operate in high-risk and challenging environments. Reconnaissance missions can be executed by these unmanned drones without endangering human operators. Drones can now function independently, make judgements based on real-time data, and perform intricate manoeuvres thanks to AI systems. Drones that are embedded with AI are also capable of adapting to evolving battlefield conditions, rendering them indispensable assets in contemporary warfare.

In addition, the field of AI algorithms for military drones is a significant area of research and development. Improved object detection, enhanced autonomous navigation, and the development of swarm technologies, which involve the coordinated operation of multiple drones, are among the advancements. Drones have become not only surveillance instruments but also essential components of advanced military tactics as a result of the integration of AI and machine learning. This has opened up fresh opportunities for military defence.

4. Algorithms at Work: The Backbone of AI Drone Functionality

AI advancements are revolutionising unmanned aerial operations, enabling drones to autonomously perform diverse tasks. Powered by sophisticated algorithms, AI transforms drones from simple aerial vehicles into intelligent agents capable of executing complex missions, adapting to environments, and making decisions.

Key to this innovation is the integration of computer vision and machine learning, allowing drones to interpret and respond to their surroundings. For instance, AI-driven surveillance drones monitor vast areas, analyse real-time data, and detect threats, making them invaluable for traffic monitoring and border security. In agriculture, drones equipped with thermal imaging and AI assess crop health, provide data on plant conditions, and deliver actionable insights for better management. Similarly, they play a crucial role in wildlife conservation by monitoring animal populations and habitats.

As drones gain autonomy, security becomes critical. Their ability to process vast data and their operational scope necessitate robust cybersecurity measures to ensure data integrity and operational safety.

5. Exploring the Use Cases of AI-Based Drones

AI-powered drones are transforming industries with diverse applications in commercial and public services. In search and rescue, these drones autonomously scan challenging terrains using object detection to locate missing persons quickly.

In urban areas, drones are integral to smart city initiatives, revolutionising logistics with drone deliveries, monitoring traffic, and supporting infrastructure maintenance. Advanced AI and machine learning enable them to navigate complex urban environments.

Environmental applications include drones equipped with sensors to monitor pollution, gather ecosystem data, and assess environmental health, aiding policy decisions. Additionally, research institutions employ drones for data collection in fields such as archaeology and climatology, opening new scientific avenues.

4.4   Intelligent Traffic Management Systems

Intelligent Traffic Management Systems (ITMS) are among the most sophisticated solutions to the congested traffic conditions that affect numerous cities. The cities transforming from rural to urban environments have also generated comparable chaos. Rapid industrialisation and urbanisation have led to many cities experiencing a growing population, resulting in unplanned city infrastructure. Unplanned infrastructures encompass "Road & Junctions, Sewerage Networks, and Utility Ducts," among others.

1. Video Traffic Detection Systems with Edge Processing Capabilities

Traffic management is susceptible to the butterfly effect, a phenomenon observed in chaotic systems like urban traffic, where a minor alteration in conditions, such as a single jaywalker, can trigger a cascading impact throughout the entire system, resulting in significant congestion across the town.

Urban planners need to have increased observation throughout the city to:

- Detect and rapidly respond to incidents.
- Get real-time information on traffic conditions.
- Proactively implement preventive measures.

It is not possible to compel everyone to adhere to the traffic regulations. However, it is possible to establish a setting in which a single casual occurrence does not halt the entire traffic system. A feasible approach to achieve this is through the implementation of connected video detection systems in key locations throughout the town. Then, integrate them with real-time traffic management systems.

Traffic Incident Management systems (TIMs) of the present day are powered by:

- Connected CCTV cameras with HD footage.
- Computer vision capabilities for image detection

and recognition.

- Edge chips for local video processing, which reduces latency.
- Cloud connectivity + GPS-based communication to receive updates.

This configuration permits the following:

a. Incidents should be detected as they occur — including car crashes, road blockages, illegal parking, and careless bike riders or pedestrians.
b. Alerts are transmitted to the intelligent traffic management system within seconds.
c. A sequence of follow-up actions can be programmed or executed automatically — emergency services can be dispatched, traffic signal controls in the area can be adjusted, public transport can be re-routed, and nearby drivers can be updated.

One of the most advantageous aspects of developing edge data processing capabilities alongside live video is the ability to repurpose the gathered data for various intelligent traffic analytics applications. The list comprises:

a. **Multimodal traffic counts:** Traffic counts across various modes to gain insight into the most frequently used methods in the area and their typical cruising speeds.
b. **Road safety analytics**: Through pattern detection,

the systems can identify and flag inappropriate behaviour from drivers and pedestrians in various locations.

c. **Programmatic alerting of response units:** Automated notifications are sent to response units, including police, ambulance services, and tow trucks or maintenance teams, upon the detection of an incident.

d. **Public transport detection**: Adaptive controls (e.g., priority passage) are implemented and on-time performance is monitored throughout the city through public transport detection.

e. **Origin–destinations traffic analysis:** In order to enhance traffic management strategies and to align controls with the most frequently encountered routes, traffic analysis is conducted between origins and destinations.

2. Advanced Safety and Pollution Analytics

A smart traffic management system is capable of much more than merely changing the traffic light to green at the appropriate moment. Designing greener and safer urban environments can also be facilitated.

These solutions can assist urban planners in achieving ambitious carbon-neutral transport goals more quickly by providing them with real-time impact data, including:

- Road infrastructure damage post-hurricane, flooding, etc.

- Air quality/pollution in the area.
- CO_2 emissions per journey.
- Dangerous driving behaviour such as harsh braking or excessive acceleration.
- Traffic throughput and speeds during different weather conditions.
- Asset performance under severe conditions — heat waves or icing.

Data can be gathered through sensors and pre-processed on edge devices. Subsequently, it may be transmitted to a cloud-based traffic centre for additional analysis. With the intelligence gathered, it is possible to implement improved policies and controls to enhance the sustainability of transportation.

3. Predictive Traffic Planning

At first glance, traffic systems might appear disordered. An experienced manager is capable of recognising repetitive patterns.

- Regular origin-destination trips
- Problematic intersections
- Narrow, congestion-prone lanes
- Overparked streets with low throughput
- And other corners of the city where navigation gets tough

An advanced traffic management system can assist in identifying troublesome areas more quickly and forecasting potential traffic congestion under specific conditions, such as during heavy snowfall, following a planned event, or due to a probable road accident.

4. Smart Junction Management

Road junctions serve as the primary points of pressure in urban areas, as they are often the sites of congestion and accidents. Again, the integration of AI algorithms and sensing technology for transportation can assist in the enhancement of safety at intersections. To achieve that, it is necessary to incorporate the following controls into intelligent traffic systems:

    a. **Turning movement counts on intersections**: This data can assist in interpreting traffic flows more effectively and optimising signals. Additionally, it can assist in understanding when and why accidents happen and in creating alternative measures to reduce the likelihood of rule violations.

    b. **Dynamic traffic light signal optimisation**: Having established numbers allows for the implementation of dynamic controls during peak times and seasonal events, while also enabling users to program custom controls in accordance with city regulations or safety planning decisions.

5. Electronic Road Pricing and Toll Collection

Optimising traffic flow is crucial for reducing congestion. This method will be inadequate if the quantity of single-occupancy vehicles on the roads continues to increase.

Up to this point, urban planners have developed two approaches aimed at decreasing the number of cars on the streets.

a. Encourage a greater number of individuals to utilise public transport through the creation of an improved transit experience centred on "Mobility as a Service (MaaS)."
b. Increase the cost associated with navigating bustling streets in a personal vehicle.

The system referred to is known as Electronic Road Pricing (ERP). Convincing individuals to opt for readily available public transport instead of private cars is a commonly employed second-level strategy. A system for enterprise resource planning depends on road infrastructure, such as cameras, gates, and gantry systems, along with in-car hardware, which may include separate devices or onboard computers, to recognise and charge vehicles entering a specific city zone.

An intelligent traffic management system is integrated with advanced versions, which generates dynamic prices for various regions based on factors such as traffic congestion, vehicle size, time of day, and other variables.

4.5   Applications in Smart Cities

Smarter and more efficient cities are being created through the implementation of Artificial Intelligence. Here are a few of the thrilling ways in which AI is revolutionising urban living.

1. Intelligent Traffic Management

Despite the potential challenges of managing traffic in densely populated urban areas, artificial intelligence can be of assistance. AI rapidly monitors traffic conditions in real-time using cameras and sensors, allowing city administrators to identify patterns and anticipate bottlenecks.

The current situation is addressed by adaptive traffic signal control, which reduces delay times and facilitates a more efficient traffic flow by modifying signals. AI also assists in the management of traffic flow by reducing pollution, saving time, and assisting vehicles in avoiding congested regions by evaluating data and suggesting the most efficient routes. The incorporation of AI technologies has resulted in a reduction in tension and an increase in efficiency in the process of driving.

2. Smart Waste Management

Despite the significant challenge of managing refuse in urban areas, artificial intelligence enhances the efficiency and intelligence of the process. AI-enabled waste collection optimisation utilises sensor data from waste receptacles to create efficient collection routes that ensure timely collection while simultaneously reducing petroleum consumption and operational expenses.

AI also enhances garbage sorting and recycling via the use

of machine learning algorithms that increase recycling rates and reduce landfill waste by recognising and separating recyclable items more efficiently than humans. AI can predict waste production patterns based on historical data, thereby facilitating the planning and administration of waste collection to prevent overflow and ensure the cleanliness of cities.

3. Energy Management and Smart Grids

Artificial intelligence is indispensable for energy management in smart cities. It encourages consumers to reduce utilisation during periods of high demand, enhances demand response initiatives, and facilitates demand forecasting. AI also facilitates the integration of renewable energy sources such as solar and wind, minimises dependence on fossil fuels, forecasts availability ensures a consistent supply, and promotes the development of eco-friendly communities.

AI also employs smart meters and sensors to collect data, analyse it to identify inefficiencies and provide recommendations for enhancements that lead to substantial energy savings and reduced carbon footprints. This optimises the utilisation of energy in commercial and residential structures. AI-powered real-time energy system monitoring and management detects errors and inefficiencies promptly, facilitating prompt resolution that guarantees a consistent energy supply, improves grid stability, and reduces downtime.

4. Public Safety and Security

Public safety and security are of the utmost importance in smart cities, and AI is significantly enhancing these areas. Artificial intelligence is the driving force behind advanced surveillance systems that instantaneously scan video streams for potential threats and anomalous activity. This enables the implementation of immediate measures and the enhancement of public safety. Additionally, AI assists law enforcement in the more effective allocation of resources and the implementation of preventative measures by utilising crime data analysis to predict crime hotspots and times.

5. Healthcare and Telemedicine

Artificial intelligence is improving the accessibility and efficacy of healthcare in smart cities by utilising predictive analytics, AI-powered services, and increased administrative efficiency. By employing AI to anticipate disease outbreaks via real-time pattern and trend detection using health data analysis, public health officials may stop the spread of diseases and take preventive measures. AI chatbots that can schedule appointments, provide medical information, and answer health-related enquiries can alleviate the burden on medical facilities and facilitate a diverse array of healthcare services, including virtual consultations and diagnostic instruments.

AI also streamlines administrative tasks, enabling healthcare professionals to focus on patient care and enhance the quality of service by organising appointments, processing insurance claims, and managing patient records.

6. Environmental Monitoring and Sustainability

In smart cities, artificial intelligence plays a critical role in monitoring and advancing environmental sustainability by improving water management, climate change mitigation, air quality monitoring, and natural resource conservation. Sensors are employed by artificial intelligence systems to monitor the integrity of the air. The collection and analysis of data on pollutants are conducted to assist local authorities in the implementation of health and environmental protection measures and to predict trends. AI is employed in water management to ensure efficient use and minimise pollution by analysing data from sensors in water systems to identify inefficiencies and leakage.

In order to mitigate climate change, AI analyses environmental data to identify regions that necessitate intervention. This enables the implementation of targeted initiatives, including the expansion of green space and the reduction of emissions. AI also guarantees sustainable use and mitigates environmental impact by monitoring consumption and identifying efficiency improvements. The utilisation of natural resources is optimised by these methods.

7. Smart Governance and Citizen Services

Artificial intelligence is revolutionising municipal government and citizen services by improving citizen involvement, decision-making, aid, and public service delivery. Chatbots and virtual assistants that are enabled by AI provide round-the-clock assistance, thereby alleviating the workload of city employees and ensuring that public aid is delivered in a timely manner. Artificial intelligence contributes to the improvement of citizen engagement by providing online platforms for the evaluation of community feedback and by assisting officials in the identification of patterns and the analysis of data.

Additionally, by automating monotonous tasks, efficiently managing public records, processing applications, and handling complaints, AI enhances the calibre, promptness, and accessibility of public services for all citizens.

8. Intelligent Transportation Systems

Using data from various modes of transportation, artificial intelligence optimises public transportation by forecasting demand, designing routes, and scheduling services. This guarantees dependability and accommodates population requirements. Artificial intelligence improves convenience and efficiency by allowing autonomous vehicles and ride-sharing applications to manage traffic and determine the most efficient routes, simultaneously reducing traffic and providing flexible transportation options.

To predictively manage transportation infrastructure,

artificial intelligence analyses sensor data from bridges, railroads, and highways. This guarantees the expeditious completion of repairs, assists in the identification of maintenance requirements, and furnishes the most recent information regarding parking availability, traffic patterns, and public transportation schedules.

9. Infrastructure and Urban Planning

Artificial intelligence significantly enhances urban planning and management by utilising predictive models, construction processes, and Geographic Information Systems (GIS). GIS helps city planners examine and analyse spatial data more efficiently, while AI can process large datasets quickly and correctly, making it easier to map land use, zoning, and infrastructure projects. Traffic patterns, population expansion, and housing demand are forecasted by artificial intelligence through historical data analysis and trend analysis.

This facilitates the efficient preparation of infrastructure and services by communities. In addition, AI facilitates "the planning, scheduling, and real-time monitoring of construction and maintenance projects". Buildings and infrastructure may be inspected by drones and robotics that are outfitted with AI to ensure timely maintenance and reduce costs.

10. Enhancing Connectivity and Communication

Artificial   intelligence   significantly   enhances communication and connection in smart cities by optimising communication infrastructures and expediting public Wi-Fi services. Artificial intelligence employs network data analysis to identify deficiencies and propose solutions, which leads to the development of robust and dependable communication systems that are essential for the management of the vast quantities of data generated by smart cities. Additionally, AI manages network traffic to ensure the seamless delivery of public Wi-Fi services, thereby ensuring the allocation of bandwidth and enabling citizens to remain connected in public spaces.

CHAPTER 5 | AI and ML in Natural Language Processing (NLP)

Learning Objective

This chapter explores the applications of AI in speech recognition, virtual assistants, text and sentiment analysis, machine translation, chatbots, and social media content monitoring.

5.1 Speech Recognition and Virtual Assistants

AI has become an integral part of the digital age, transforming industries and redefining how humans interact with technology. Among its many applications, speech recognition and virtual assistants stand out as revolutionary technologies that have permeated daily life. These advancements are the result of years of research and development, blending machine learning, Natural Language Processing (NLP), and computational linguistics to create seamless, intelligent, and user-friendly systems.

5.1.1 AI in Speech Recognition

The process of identifying a human voice is referred to as speech recognition. Firms typically create these programs and integrate them into various hardware devices to detect speech. When the software receives a command or hears a voice, it will respond appropriately.

Voice recognition software is developed by numerous organisations that implement state-of-the-art technologies, including artificial intelligence, machine learning, and neural networks. Technologies such as "Cortana," "Alexa," "Siri," and "Google Assistant" have revolutionised how individuals interact with electronics and technology. A variety of items are included, such as automobiles, cell phones, and home security systems.

Don't forget that speech and voice recognition are distinct concepts. The process of speech recognition involves the initial identification of spoken words in an audio recording of a speaker, which is then translated into text. In contrast, speech recognition is limited to the identification of pre-programmed spoken instructions.

1. Developing Knowledge of Speech Recognition

Speech recognition technology, also referred to as Automatic Speech Recognition (ASR), enables Artificial Intelligence (AI) systems and computers to convert spoken words into text. Several stages are involved in this process:

a. **Decoding:** The final stage involves selecting the most likely translation for the spoken words, as determined by the data collected during the preceding procedures.

b. **Feature extraction:** This stage involves the processing of the audio input to extract characteristics, including Mel-Frequency Cepstral Coefficients (MFCCs), which provide the system with the requisite information to identify the sound.

c. **Acoustic Analysis:** The system first captures the audio signal, which is subsequently dissected into its constituent elements, including prosody and phonemes.

d. **Language Modelling:** To enhance the accuracy of recognition, language models are employed to understand the semantics as well as the grammatical structure of spoken words.

e. **Acoustic Modelling:** Statistical models are implemented by the system to establish a connection between the retrieved characteristics and the recognised phonetic patterns and language context.

2. Parts of AI Speech Recognition

Speech recognition in AI, or Automatic Speech Recognition (ASR), is a sophisticated technique that enables machines to convert spoken language into text or other comprehensible forms. Some numerous components and stages comprise speech recognition technology:

a. **Audio Input:** Audio input is typically recorded using a microphone, which initiates the procedure. Commands and conversations, as well as any spoken human discourse, may serve as this aural input.

b. **Preprocessing:** It is necessary to preprocess the unprocessed audio signal to improve its fidelity and prepare it for analysis. Noise reduction, signal amplification, or other techniques may be implemented to enhance the audio data.

c. **Language Modelling:** The grammatical structure and semantics of spoken words are understood via the use of language models. These models improve the system's word recognition accuracy by helping it comprehend the context and relationships between words. Language modelling plays a critical role in handling homophones, which are words that sound the same but have different meanings, as well as changes in word order and sentence structure.

d. **Decoding:** In order to decipher the spoken words, the system combines the information from the linguistic and acoustic models. Based on statistical probability, it evaluates numerous word combinations and ascertains the transcription that is most plausible.

e. **Output:** The ultimate output is a command or recognised language that can be applied to a variety of situations. This output has the potential to be employed for a variety of duties, including transcription, device operation, and virtual assistant instruction.

3.   Applications of AI for Speech Recognition

For speech recognition, artificial intelligence is employed as a commercial solution in numerous domains and applications. Artificial intelligence's enhanced accuracy in data transcription and its more natural user interactions with hardware and software are advantageous to voice-activated audio content assistants, call centres, ATMs, and other applications.

a.   **Telecommunications:** Call management and analysis are more efficient with speech recognition models. Achieving superior customer service allows agents to concentrate on their most valuable skills. The availability of voice transcription services and text messaging has enabled customers to communicate with companies in real-time, 24 hours a day. This has improved their overall experience and has heightened their sense of connection with the company.

b.   **Medical:** Voice-activated artificial intelligence is increasingly prevalent in the telecommunications sector. More efficient call management and analysis are achieved through speech recognition technology models. Achieving superior customer service allows agents to concentrate on their most valuable skills.

c.   **Banking:** Financial and banking organisations employ AI applications to assist clients with their business enquiries. A bank can be approached for details regarding the current interest rate of a savings account or the balance of the account. With the elimination of the need for in-depth research or access to cloud data, customer service representatives can respond to requests more quickly and provide exceptional assistance.

d. **Automotive Voice Commands:** Hands-free voice control of conveniences such as navigation, entertainment systems, and climate control is a prevalent feature of contemporary automobiles.

5.1.2 AI in Virtual Assistants

An application program that comprehends natural language voice commands and performs tasks for the individual is known as a virtual assistant, AI assistant, or digital assistant. These tasks, which were traditionally carried out by a human personal assistant or secretary, encompass activities such as taking dictation, reading text or email messages aloud, searching for phone numbers, scheduling, making phone calls and reminding the individual about appointments.

In contrast to conventional automation tools, these assistants possess the ability to comprehend context, learn from interactions, and modify their responses to enhance efficiency.

A wide variety of services can be provided by virtual assistants, including:

a. Offering details such as weather updates, and facts from various sources like Wikipedia or IMDb, as well as the ability to set alarms, create to-do lists, and compile shopping lists.

b. Engaging with music through streaming platforms such as Spotify and Pandora, tuning into radio stations, and listening to audiobooks.

c. Watching videos, television shows, or films on screens, streaming from platforms such as Netflix.

1. AI Virtual Assistant in the Workplace

In the current rapid business landscape, the importance of efficiency and productivity cannot be overstated. Virtual assistants powered by AI provide a means to automate tasks that are repetitive and consume a lot of time. This enables the workforce to concentrate on strategic initiatives and creativity instead of routine administrative tasks.

With the evolution of technology, it is anticipated that these assistants will become increasingly integrated into routines, influencing the future of personal and professional productivity. Some of the advanced features of AI-driven personal assistants are highlighted here:

a. **Natural Language Understanding:** In AI assistants, Natural Language Understanding (NLU) denotes the capability of computer software to grasp and interpret human language as a whole, rather than merely focusing on single words. AI assistants are enabled to analyse the sentiments, intentions, and implications behind a speaker's statement, which allows for more natural and human-like interactions.

b. **Context Awareness:** The virtual assistants can analyse contextual information to deliver relevant and personalised responses. User preferences can be understood, allowing for behaviour adaptation accordingly.

c. **Multi-Platform Integration:** Personal assistants powered by AI can integrate effortlessly with a range of platforms and devices, such as smartphones, smart speakers, and smart home systems. This facilitates a smooth and cohesive experience for users.

d. **Voice Recognition:** Voice recognition serves as an essential element of AI assistants, enabling them to comprehend and interpret spoken instructions from individuals. Voice recognition software captures spoken commands and converts them into text, which is subsequently analysed by natural language processing algorithms to comprehend the user's intent.

e. **Task Automation:** Through the utilisation of sophisticated algorithms and machine learning capabilities, AI technology enables organisations to automate internal processes. Employee morale and retention are improved, and job satisfaction is increased, as repetitive and mundane duties are transferred to AI systems, allowing employees to concentrate on more engaging and taxing work.

Task automation driven by AI can include various features and capabilities, such as automated email responses through natural language processing, interactions with chatbots, and recognition of voice commands.

2. Underlying Technologies:

The major technologies that underlie AI virtual assistance are as follows:

a. **Natural Language Processing (NLP):** The component of the system enables AI assistants to "listen" and "understand" human language, regardless of whether it is spoken or typed. This allows the assistant to handle requests in a manner similar to that of a human.

b. **Machine Learning (ML):** AI assistants become smarter over time due to machine learning. The assistant takes note of the user's interactions and adjusts to their habits. It essentially adapts to individual preferences to provide improved service over time.

c. **Automation:** The action step involves automation. After comprehending the request, the assistant carries out the task by engaging with various systems or tools. This occurs in mere seconds without the need for manual checks or detail input.

3. Applications of AI Virtual Assistants

Artificial intelligence virtual assistants are devised to execute an extensive array of functions that enhance productivity and facilitate routine duties. The following are a few of the most prevalent and practical applications:

a. Scheduling

AI assistants are highly proficient in organising schedules. They can be asked to arrange meetings, send calendar invitations, or provide reminders for significant events. An example would be instructing the assistant to arrange a team meeting for Friday at 10 AM, which leads to the assistant checking the availability of all members and sending out invitations effortlessly.

b. Communication Assistance

AI assistants can assist in streamlining communication, from drafting emails to sending quick messages. Lengthy email threads can be summarised, responses can be suggested, and customer queries can be handled in real-time, eliminating the need for manual typing of repetitive messages.

c. Information Retrieval

Information can be fetched from databases, files, or even the web by AI assistants. For instance, enquiring about the revenue for Q3 will prompt the assistant to retrieve the pertinent report and provide a summary of the data.

d. Task Automation

AI assistants can effortlessly manage routine duties such as setting reminders, creating to-do lists, and following up on deadlines. For instance, an assistant can serve as a reminder to submit a report each Friday without necessitating a new command each week.

e. Customer Support

Chatbots and virtual agents powered by AI serve as the initial support for companies. Common customer enquiries, such as "Where is my order?" or "How do I reset my password?" can be handled effectively. This leads to quicker replies and allows human agents to focus on more intricate problems.

f. Data Analysis and Reporting

AI assistants possess the ability to analyse data and produce reports. For instance, tracking the team's weekly performance can yield insights such as, "The team completed 90% of assigned tasks this week, showing a 10% improvement compared to the previous week."

g. Personal Assistance

On a more personal level, these assistants can aid individuals in organising their lives beyond the workplace. Weather updates can be provided, appointments can be booked, and smart home devices can be managed, such as turning off the lights or adjusting the thermostat.

5.2   Text Analysis and Sentiment Analysis

Text analytics frequently accompanies sentiment analysis in the process of monitoring customer feedback. Both elements are crucial for a successful program in customer experience management, as they enable the extraction of meaningful insights from the data collected regarding customers.

1. Text Analytics

Text Analytics involves the use of statistical and machine learning methods to predict, prescribe, or infer information from data that has been mined from text.

Analysing textual data, including emails, social media interactions, and chats, presents challenges due to the absence of structure within the data. Sorting through text manually is both time-consuming and costly, particularly when there is a need to enlist extra assistance for the task.

Automatic extraction of useful information from unstructured text data can be achieved through text analytics, which is a machine learning technique. Organisations utilise text analytics tools to swiftly process web data and documents, transforming them into valuable insights.

Text analysis techniques are classified into various categories:

a. **Text Classification:** The text is organised into specific classes or categories according to its content or characteristics.

b. **Text Extraction:** Identifies and extracts specific elements of a larger text for further analysis or summarization.

c. **Word Frequency:** It calculates the frequency of each word in a text or a set of texts, offering insights into the most prevalent or important words utilised.

d. **Word Sense Disambiguation:** Establishes the accurate meaning or interpretation of a word within a specific context, as numerous words may possess various meanings.

e. **Clustering:** Documents or data points are grouped together according to their content similarity.

2. Sentiment Analysis

Sentiment analysis, which is also referred to as opinion mining or emotion AI, is a method that employs biometrics, computational linguistics, text analysis, and natural language processing to systematically identify, extract, quantify, and investigate subjective information and affective states.

The process of sentiment analysis involves assessing whether a piece of writing, like a consumer product review, conveys a positive or negative tone. Numerous business organisations are progressively depending on sentiment analysis to evaluate their brand's reputation and gain insights into their customers.

Here are a few categories of sentiment analysis techniques:

a. **Graded Sentiment Analysis:** Assesses the sentiment of a text using a scale ranging from 1 to 5 to indicate the strength of the emotion conveyed.

b. **Emotion Detection:** Recognises and classifies the particular emotions conveyed in a text, including joy, sorrow, rage, anxiety, and others.

c. **Aspect-based Sentiment Analysis:** It assesses the sentiment by analysing specific entities within the text data, offering a more detailed comprehension of opinions and emotions associated with various aspects.

d. **Multilingual Sentiment Analysis:** Identifies the sentiment expressed in texts composed in various languages.

3. **The Differences between Text and Sentiment Analysis**

There are the following important differences between sentiment analysis and text analytics:

a. **Early warning signs:** Through text analytics, it is possible to receive an alert when a new topic emerges within the data. For instance, examining feedback for a restaurant may reveal a sudden rise in the use of the word "spoilt," prompting a swift investigation into that matter. A decline in sentiment score indicates that a certain aspect of the business has resulted in customer dissatisfaction.

b. **Analyse different kinds of content:** Monitoring the topics that are being discussed, the issues that are receiving the most attention, and the individuals who are contributing the most to the conversation is possible. Sentiment analysis can be utilised for non-text content like video, audio, and imagery to uncover the positivity or negativity of the content, as a smile conveys a higher sentiment score compared to a scowl.

c. **Different internal workings:** Text analysis tools utilise Natural Language Processing (NLP) technology to handle text-based data similarly to how the human brain interprets language. Through the use of unique algorithms, it recognises the different elements of speech, understands the relationships between words and concepts, automatically rectifies errors, and extracts meaning. It can closely examine a single tweet to identify the fundamental patterns and trends. Sentiment analysis explores the implications of words and phrases, determining if they convey positive or negative sentiments. Understanding the customer's feelings can be enhanced by discussing each subtopic individually.

5.3 Machine Translation Systems

Machine translation is a branch of computational linguistics that concentrates on the creation of systems that are capable of autonomously translating text or speech from one language to another. Machine translation in Natural Language Processing (NLP) is designed to generate translations that accurately convey the original content's meaning while also being grammatically correct.

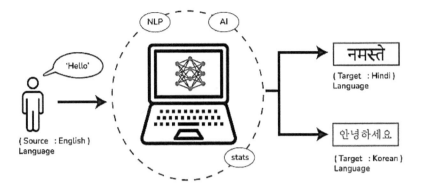

Figure 5.1 Machine Translation Model.

1. Approaches in Machine Translation

In machine translation, the source text is first decoded and then encoded into the target language using a two-step process that incorporates several strategies used by language translation technologies to speed up the translation process.

a) Rule-Based Machine Translation

Relying on these resources, rule-based machine translation guarantees the accurate translation of particular content. The process entails the software parsing the input text, producing a transitional representation, and subsequently converting it into the target language using grammar rules and dictionaries.

---

*https://media.geeksforgeeks.org/wp-content/uploads/20231226141038/Machine-Translation-Model.png

b) Statistical Machine Translation

Text translation is accomplished through statistical machine translation, which employs machine learning rather than linguistic norms. Extensive human translations are analysed by machine learning algorithms to identify statistical patterns. The program makes educated assumptions when given a new source text to translate by considering the statistical probability that certain words or phrases will be linked to other words or phrases in the destination language.

c) Neural Machine Translation (NMT)

A network of interconnected elements that functions as an information system is known as a neural network, and is inspired by the human brain. An output is generated by the transmission of input data through these nodes. Neural networks are used by neural machine translation software to handle large datasets. Until the output node receives the final result, each node contributes a distinct modification from source text to destination text.

d) Hybrid Machine Translation

In order to optimise the efficiency of a single translation model, hybrid machine translation tools incorporate multiple machine translation models into a single software application. This approach is a combination of methodologies. This procedure typically entails the integration of statistical and rule-based machine translation subsystems, with the final translation output being a composite of the results produced by each subsystem.

2. Benefits of Machine Translation in NLP

Several benefits are associated with machine translation in "Natural Language Processing (NLP)," such as:

a. **Improved communication:** Language barriers are dismantled and international cooperation is facilitated by machine translation, which simplifies communication between individuals who speak different languages.

b. **Cost savings:** For businesses and organisations that require the translation of substantial volumes of text, machine translation is a cost-effective solution that is generally more efficient and less expensive than human translation.

c. **Increased accessibility:** Machine translation can enhance the user experience and broaden the dissemination of digital products and services by increasing the accessibility of digital content to users who speak different languages.

d. **Improved efficiency:** In addition to enhancing overall efficacy, machine translation can also simplify the translation process, enabling businesses and organisations to rapidly translate substantial volumes of text.

e. **Language learning:** A valuable aid for language learners, machine translation can assist them in comprehending the meaning of unfamiliar terms and phrases and enhancing their language skills.

3. Application of Machine Translation

The applications of machine translation are numerous, such as:

a. **Cross-border communication:** Machine translation facilitates international cooperation by enabling individuals from diverse countries to communicate more readily, thereby dismantling language barriers.

b. **Localisation:** The utilisation of machine translation can facilitate the rapid and efficient translation of websites, software, and other digital content into various languages, thereby increasing their accessibility to users worldwide.

c. **Business:** Businesses may leverage machine translation to translate contracts, documents, and other critical materials, thereby facilitating collaboration with consumers and partners worldwide.

d. **Education:** Machine translation has the potential to enhance the language abilities of students and facilitate the acquisition of new languages in the field of education.

e. **Government:** Machine translation can be implemented by governments to enhance transparency and accessibility by translating official documents and communications.

5.4   Chatbots and Conversational AI

A chatbot is software that mimics human-like interaction when engaging customers in conversation, while conversational AI represents a wider technology that allows computers to replicate conversations, encompassing both chatbots and virtual assistants.

1.   Understanding Chatbot

A chatbot is a computer program designed to simulate human conversations with users using Artificial Intelligence (AI). One of the most prevalent types of chatbots comprehends the words, phrases, and context of the conversation to execute basic duties and respond to enquiries. Specific duties, including flight reservations, food ordering, and online purchasing, are frequently the extent of these fundamental chatbots.

Two types of chatbots exist: rule-based chatbots and AI-based chatbots.

  a. **Rule-based chatbots:** They depend on set responses to enquiries and do not gain knowledge from interactions with people. They can respond with pre-fabricated responses that are initiated by specific keywords or phrases. Rule-based chatbots cannot respond to new enquiries or when users express something unexpected.

  b. **AI-based chatbots:** Utilise artificial intelligence to develop a deeper understanding of the requirements of their users over time and to respond intelligently in accordance with those needs by learning from interactions with humans. AI chatbots can learn from earlier conversations and adjust according to the insights gained from prior interactions with individuals.

2. Understanding Conversational AI

Conversational AI enables chatbots to comprehend human language and respond appropriately. Conversational AI allows the chatbot to respond in a natural manner.

The system employs speech recognition and machine learning to comprehend what individuals are expressing, their emotional states, the context of the conversation, and how to respond suitably. Additionally, it offers support for various communication channels, such as voice, text, and video, and possesses context awareness, enabling comprehension of intricate requests that involve multiple inputs and outputs.

The essential distinction between chatbots and conversational AI lies in the fact that the former refers to a computer program, while the latter represents a category of technology. Some examples of conversational AI chatbots are Siri, Cortana, and Alexa. A chatbot's ability to utilise conversational AI technology varies based on its level of sophistication.

A chatbot that is trained with Natural Language Processing (NLP), possesses context awareness and can comprehend multiple intents qualifies as a conversational AI chatbot. Businesses often leverage chatbots to assist in achieving specific marketing, sales, or support objectives, and their success is monitored through metrics like goal completion rate.

There are three kinds of conversational AI applications, and they are:

a. **Chatbots:** Chatbots utilise conversational AI to mimic a dialogue with a human being. Not all chatbots utilise conversational AI; however, those that do generally deliver a more natural and relevant output, as they are trained with Natural Language Processing (NLP) models.

b. **Voice assistants:** These are software programs that execute tasks according to voice commands. This system employs language processing algorithms, vocal recognition, and voice synthesis to comprehend the command and generate the required outputs. Examples include Amazon's Alexa, Apple's Siri, and Microsoft's Cortana.

c. **Virtual assistants:** These chatbots are powered by AI and possess context awareness, assisting users in completing specific tasks. These systems are driven by NLP and Natural Language Understanding (NLU) models, resulting in output that is more personalised, accurate, and engaging.

Differences between Chatbots and Conversational AI

Chatbots and conversational AI are frequently mentioned in tandem, yet recognising their distinctions is crucial. It is imperative to acquire a comprehensive comprehension of these distinctions to identify the most suitable solution for unique needs.

Chatbots	Conversational AI
Capable of text-only commands, inputs, and outputs.	Capable of voice and text commands, inputs and outputs.
Single channel: can be used as a chat interface only.	Omnichannel: can be deployed on websites, voice assistants, smart speakers, and call centres.
Pre-determined scripted conversational flow.	Natural language processing, understanding and contextualisation.
Rule-based, canned linear interactions. Cannot handle out-of-scope tasks.	Wide-scope, non-linear, dynamic interactions.
Navigational focused	Dialogue focused
Any update or revision to the pre-defined rules and conversational flow demands reconfiguration.	Continual learning and fast iteration cycles.
Manual maintenance, updates and revisions =	Highly scalable. As the company's database and

difficult and time-consuming to scale.	pages are updated, so does the conversational AI interface.
Time-consuming and complicated building process.	Easy deployment and integration with existing databases, and text corpora.

5.5   AI in Social Media Content Monitoring

Social media monitoring that is AI-based involves the automatic monitoring, analysis, and response to brand mentions, keywords, phrases, or behaviours across a variety of social media platforms. This entails the exploitation of AI capabilities, including Natural Language Processing (NLP) for the comprehension of human language, Machine Learning for the prediction of trends and user behaviours, and image recognition for the analysis of visual content.

The automation of data acquisition, analysis, and interpretation is a critical component of social media surveillance, which is facilitated by AI. It enables businesses to monitor consumer sentiment, identifies emergent trends, and trace brand mentions in real-time, thereby facilitating strategic planning and proactive decision-making.

1.   Benefits of AI Social Media Monitoring

The primary benefits of AI Social Media Monitoring include the following:

a) Real-Time Insights

Real-time insights into market trends and customer conversations are among the primary advantages of AI social media monitoring. Businesses can maintain a competitive edge and expedite their responses to emergent opportunities or issues by consistently monitoring social media channels.

b) Improved Customer Engagement

Businesses can more effectively interact with consumers by identifying and promptly responding to their needs and concerns through the use of AI-powered social media monitoring tools. Companies can customise their responses to correspond with the tone and sentiment of consumer interactions by employing sentiment analysis and Natural Language Processing (NLP) techniques.

c) Crisis Management

AI social media monitoring can be invaluable in preventing harm to a company's reputation in the event of a crisis or negative publicity. Businesses can maintain consumer trust and manage the situation by promptly identifying and addressing negative sentiment or misinformation.

d) Competitor Analysis

Valuable insights into competitors' strategies and activities are also provided by AI social media monitoring tools.

Businesses can benchmark their performance, identify market gaps, and maintain a competitive edge by monitoring competitor mentions, engagement metrics, and sentiment analysis.

2. Working of AI Social Media Monitoring

The following is a discussion of the workings of AI in social media monitoring:

a) Data Collection

Data is collected from a variety of sources, such as public social media platforms, blogs, news websites, and forums, by AI social media monitoring tools. Finally, the data is aggregated and processed to derive pertinent information, including brand mentions, keywords, and trends.

b) Natural Language Processing (NLP)

NLP is a branch of artificial intelligence that concentrates on the interaction between human languages and computers. In the context of social media surveillance, NLP algorithms are employed to analyse and comprehend the meaning of text-based content, including social media posts, remarks, and reviews.

c) Sentiment Analysis

Sentiment analysis is a critical element of AI social media monitoring, which enables businesses to evaluate the general sentiment of consumer conversations and feedback. Businesses can detect emergent issues, identify trends, and accurately assess customer satisfaction levels by categorising text as positive, negative, or neutral.

d) Trend Detection

Artificial intelligence social media monitoring tools employ sophisticated algorithms to identify emergent trends and topics of discussion on a variety of social media platforms. Through the examination of trends in user behaviour and content interaction, companies may spot chances for marketing campaigns, content production, and new product development.

CHAPTER 6

AI and ML in Manufacturing and Industry

Learning Objective

This chapter examines the use of AI and ML in predictive maintenance, quality control, automation, smart manufacturing, supply chain optimisation, and energy efficiency in industry.

6.1 Predictive Maintenance Using AI

Predictive maintenance, which employs data, technology, and analytical tools to anticipate potential equipment or apparatus malfunctions, is a proactive approach to asset management.

Businesses can avoid unexpected failures, streamline maintenance schedules, and extend the life of assets by performing timely maintenance. By employing these strategies, operational efficiency is improved and costs are significantly reduced in a variety of sectors.

In industries that depend on equipment reliability, such as manufacturing, energy, aviation, healthcare, and transportation, predictive maintenance marks a transition from conventional reactive methods to a proactive, data-informed approach. This is especially important. This modification significantly enhances cost management, reliability, and efficiency.

1.   Applications of AI in Predictive Maintenance

In a variety of industries, AI has a wide range of applications in predictive maintenance, where it enhances operational efficiency and equipment reliability by utilising its capabilities in data analysis, machine learning, and predictive analytics. Some of the most significant applications are mentioned below:

a)   Predictive failure analysis

The analysis of historical equipment data to predict potential malfunctions is a valuable application of AI in predictive maintenance. By recognising patterns, trends, and early warning signs, organisations can proactively schedule maintenance, thereby minimising unplanned downtime and production interruptions. The reliability and efficacy of critical assets in a variety of industries are improved by this method, which optimises resource allocation and reduces maintenance costs.

b)   Anomaly detection

AI's anomaly detection, a critical application, entails the continuous surveillance of sensor data from apparatus and equipment to identify deviations from usual operating conditions. The maintenance teams are notified by the system when anomalies are detected, allowing them to resolve prospective issues before they result in failures. Industry sectors that prioritise uninterrupted production, reliability, and safety, including healthcare, aviation, and manufacturing, are particularly advantageous to this application.

c) Optimal maintenance scheduling

AI is redefining the planning and execution of maintenance in predictive maintenance. AI algorithms establish maintenance schedules that are dynamically determined by operational criticality, resource availability, equipment conditions, and production schedules, as opposed to reactive measures or fixed schedules. By guaranteeing that maintenance is executed precisely when required, this methodology minimises operational disruptions, reduces expenses, and prolongs asset lifespans.

d) Condition-based monitoring

Using real-time data from sensors and monitoring systems, this method evaluates the performance and condition of the equipment. In contrast to fixed-time maintenance, condition-based monitoring customises maintenance activities to the equipment's current condition, issuing alerts when specific thresholds are achieved. A data-driven approach that improves operational efficiency and reduces maintenance costs, this method optimises resource use, minimises delay, and maintains assets in optimal condition.

e) Prescriptive maintenance

An advanced implementation of AI in predictive maintenance, prescriptive maintenance not only forecasts the necessity of maintenance but also recommends specific actions to rectify identified issues. Simple duties, such as software updates, may be recommended, as well as intricate repairs. In industries where equipment reliability is critical, this method is indispensable, as it optimises resource allocation, minimises unplanned outages, reduces maintenance costs, and reduces maintenance expenses.

f) Asset health score

AI algorithms assess equipment conditions by analysing multiple parameters and historical data to generate a quantitative asset health score. This enables organisations to prioritise maintenance by focusing on critical assets, improving efficiency, minimising disruptions, and reducing costs in sectors reliant on asset reliability.

g) Root cause analysis

Predictive maintenance's root cause analysis endeavours to identify the fundamental causes of equipment malfunctions by examining historical data and historical patterns. This method, in contrast to applications that anticipate the necessity of maintenance, assists in comprehending the reasons for failures, thereby facilitating the development of targeted solutions and preventative measures to mitigate future complications.

This approach is essential in industries that require reliability and disruption. It is data-driven.

h) Energy efficiency optimisation

However, this AI application extends beyond predictive maintenance to optimise energy consumption in operations and facilities. AI assesses energy utilisation patterns and equipment performance data to identify opportunities for energy savings, suggesting modifications to decrease consumption. In industries with substantial energy expenditures, this is advantageous, as it aligns with environmental and regulatory objectives and yields cost savings.

i) Prognostics and Health Management (PHM)

AI techniques, including prognostic modelling, assist in the estimation of the Remaining Useful Life (RUL) of apparatus components or systems. AI can forecast the health status of assets by examining historical performance data and degradation patterns, thereby enabling maintenance teams to develop proactive interventions and prevent unforeseen failures.

j) Remote monitoring and diagnostics

Remote monitoring systems powered by AI enable real-time monitoring of equipment performance from any location, enabling maintenance teams to remotely identify issues and implement timely corrective actions. AI is capable of efficiently troubleshooting issues by utilising sophisticated diagnostics capabilities, thereby reducing the necessity for onsite inspections and minimising disruption.

2.   Benefits of AI-Powered Predictive Maintenance

AI-powered predictive maintenance provides organisations in a variety of industries with a plethora of advantages. Each of these benefits contributes to enhanced reliability, reduced costs, and improved operational efficiency. Here are the primary benefits of predictive maintenance powered by AI:

a. **Improved asset uptime:** AI-powered predictive maintenance assists in the prevention of unforeseen failures by detecting issues before their escalation. This ensures that apparatus and machinery are accessible when required for operations, increasing asset utilisation.

b. **Reduced maintenance costs:** AI-driven predictive maintenance focuses resources on apparatus that legitimately requires attention, thereby optimising maintenance schedules. The overall maintenance workload is reduced, and the costs associated with superfluous restorations and part replacements are reduced.

c. **Enhanced safety and reliability:** AI-powered systems can improve workplace safety and guarantee the reliability of equipment by proactively addressing maintenance requirements. This lessens the likelihood of accidents and expensive equipment malfunctions, particularly in industries that involve hazardous operations.

d. **Minimised unplanned downtime:** Organisations can reduce the interruptions to production or services by scheduling maintenance during scheduled idleness, which is facilitated by the capacity to anticipate equipment malfunctions. This leads to a reduction in the number of unanticipated downtime incidents, which can be both disruptive and expensive.

e. **Better resource allocation:** Organisations can apportion resources more efficiently by utilising predictive maintenance, which offers insights into the timing and nature of necessary maintenance activity. Tasks may be ranked by maintenance teams according to asset condition, resource availability, and criticality.

f. **Extended asset lifespan:** The tenure of costly assets can be extended through predictive maintenance, which addresses issues before their progression to severe damage. This holds particular significance in sectors that necessitate substantial capital expenditures, including aviation and manufacturing.

g. **Optimised spare parts inventory:** Artificial intelligence-driven maintenance systems are capable of accurately predicting the likelihood of specific components or elements failing. Organisations can reduce the need for excess stock and associated transportation costs by maintaining an optimised spare parts inventory.

h. **Real-time monitoring and alerts:** Many predictive maintenance solutions that are powered by AI provide real-time monitoring and alerts. Immediate notifications are sent to maintenance teams when an asset's condition declines, facilitating prompt intervention.

i. **Energy efficiency:** Energy utilisation can be optimised through predictive maintenance in conjunction with AI. It can detect equipment inefficiencies and suggest modifications to decrease energy consumption, resulting in cost savings and environmental advantages.

j. **Data-driven decision-making:** Providing organisations with data-driven insights, predictive maintenance is based on machine learning and data analytics. This encourages the process of continuous development in maintenance practices and the ability to make informed decisions.

3. Components of AI-Based Predictive Maintenance

Predictive maintenance (PdM) that is AI-based is composed of several critical components that facilitate the efficient surveillance of equipment health and the prediction of potential malfunctions in a variety of industries. The following is a flexible breakdown of these components:

a) **Sensors**: Diverse parameters, including temperature, pressure, and performance metrics, are collected in real-time by these devices, which are positioned strategically. It is the foundation of predictive maintenance analysis that sensor data is used to provide insights into the health of apparatus or assets.

b) **Data preprocessing**: Raw sensor data frequently contains inconsistencies and noise. In order to guarantee that predictive modelling is accurate, data preprocessing involves the cleansing, normalisation, and management of absent data to ensure that the data is of high quality.

c) **AI algorithms**: Preprocessed data is analysed by these algorithms, which employ machine learning and deep learning techniques to identify significant features that are associated with potential malfunctions. By analysing historical data patterns, they can forecast apparatus failures, anomalies, and Remaining Useful Life (RUL) in a variety of industrial conditions.

d) **Decision-making modules**: Determining the necessity of maintenance actions is the responsibility of decision-making modules, which process insights generated by AI algorithms. When intervention is necessary, these modules notify the appropriate systems or individuals, schedule maintenance tasks, and suggest preventative or corrective maintenance operations.

e) **Communication and integration**: This element guarantees the seamless integration and communication of insights from the PdM system across a variety of stakeholders and systems within an organisation. The process entails the integration of enterprise systems such as ERP and asset management software, as well as the interaction with maintenance teams and management. It is tailored to the unique requirements of various industries.

f) **User interface and reporting**: Reporting tools and user interfaces are indispensable for facilitating accessibility and decision-making. Regardless of the industry, these tools enable users to comprehend intricate data patterns and make informed decisions by offering data visualisation, dashboard, and reporting capabilities. Visual aids facilitate the dissemination of forecast information and data insights to pertinent parties.

6.2　Machine Learning for Quality Control

Quality control is essential in the manufacturing process, as it guarantees that products satisfy customer expectations and adhere to the desired standards. Machine learning has emerged as a potent instrument to transform quality control processes as technology continues to advance. Manufacturing companies can enhance their efficiency, accuracy, and overall quality control measures by utilising data and algorithms to facilitate machine learning.

1. Machine Learning Applications in Quality Control

There are numerous applications of machine learning in the field of quality control in manufacturing. One critical application is the identification and classification of defects. By automating the detection and classification of defects, manufacturers can reduce human error and enhance efficiency by training machine learning algorithms on extensive datasets that encompass both defective and non-defective products.

Utilising predictive maintenance is an additional application. Patterns indicative of potential malfunctions can be identified by machine learning algorithms through the analysis of sensor data from Machinery and Equipment. Manufacturers can proactively schedule maintenance, which reduces production interruptions and enhances the overall efficacy of their equipment.

Moreover, machine learning has the potential to enhance quality control by optimising manufacturing processes. To identify variables that influence product quality, machine learning algorithms analyse data from a variety of sources, such as supplier data and production data. In this way, manufacturers can enhance their production processes and make data-driven decisions.

2. Benefits of Machine Learning in Quality Control

Many benefits are associated with the integration of machine learning into quality control:

a) Improved Accuracy

Patterns that may be challenging for humans to identify can be identified by machine learning algorithms, which are capable of analysing vast datasets.

The accuracy of quality control is enhanced by machine learning, which accurately identifies defects or abnormalities in manufacturing processes. This ultimately results in an improvement in the overall quality of the products by reducing the number of false positives and false negatives.

b) Enhanced Efficiency

Machine learning automates quality control processes, thereby streamlining decision-making and reducing manual labour. Machine learning algorithms are capable of rapidly identifying potential issues and implementing corrective measures through the processing and analysis of large volumes of data in real-time. Decreasing downtime and enabling manufacturers to promptly resolve quality control concerns enhances efficiency.

c) Predictive Maintenance

Machine learning algorithms can predict equipment failures by analysing sensor data. The proactive scheduling of maintenance by manufacturers can reduce unplanned outages and enhance the overall efficacy of equipment by identifying patterns and anomalies. In turn, this leads to enhanced production efficiency and cost savings.

d) Data-Driven Decision Making

Data-driven decision-making is facilitated by machine learning, which offers valuable insights for quality and control. Manufacturers can ensure that their processes are optimised and that product quality is improved by analysing a vast quantity of data, such as production data, supplier data, and customer feedback. This results in enhanced overall quality control and more effective resource allocation.

e) Real-Time Monitoring

In real-time, machine learning algorithms can perpetually monitor manufacturing processes, enabling the immediate identification of anomalies or defects. In order to prevent defective products from accessing the market, manufacturers can promptly implement corrective measures and provide real-time insights. Additionally, real-time monitoring minimises the possible effect on production by enabling a quicker reaction to any violations of quality requirements.

3. Challenges of Machine Learning in Quality Control

Challenges are associated with the implementation of machine learning in quality control:

a) Data Availability and Quality

To implement machine learning in quality control, it is necessary to have access to extensive, high-quality datasets. A machine learning algorithm's accuracy and efficacy may be compromised by inadequate or insufficient data. In order to train algorithms effectively, manufacturers must ensure that proper labelling and the collection of relevant and reliable data are completed.

b) Cost and Resources

Significant resources, such as the infrastructure necessary to manage and process large volumes of data, as well as specialised expertise to create and sustain the algorithms, may be necessary for the successful implementation of machine learning. The expenses associated with the acquisition and maintenance of these resources can pose a challenge for certain organisations, particularly lesser manufacturers.

c) Continuous Training and Adaptation

The continuous training and refining of machine learning models is necessary to accommodate changes in customer requirements, new types of defects, or evolving production processes. In order to guarantee that the algorithms continue to be accurate and effective over time, it is necessary to continuously acquire and label data, retrain the models, and maintain their accuracy.

d) Interpretability and Explainability

Despite its superiority in spotting trends and forecasting outcomes, machine learning algorithms are often seen as "black boxes," which makes it challenging to comprehend and analyse the decision-making process. This lack of interpretability may be problematic for quality control as producers must defend and explain the algorithms' choices, particularly when there are audits or consumer complaints.

e) Ethical and Legal Considerations

Machine learning systems are dependent on the data they are trained on, and any biases or inaccuracies in the data can affect the impartiality and legality of the decisions it makes. To guarantee ethical and legal conformance in quality control processes, it is essential to carefully evaluate the accountability of algorithmic decisions and the potential biases in the data.

6.3   Automation and Smart Manufacturing

The pursuit of cost optimisation, superior product quality, and increased productivity has been a consistent trend in the ever-changing manufacturing landscape. This revolution in "Smart Manufacturing" has provided manufacturers with unparalleled opportunities to achieve these objectives with remarkable success. The power of industrial AI and ML is at the core of this transformative wave.

The cost of capturing and storing data has decreased, and it has become a valuable asset in the current digital era. The extraordinary capabilities of AI and ML are enabling manufacturers in a variety of industries to leverage the potential of this data to transform their operations and increase their profitability. Manufacturers can improve production efficiency and resolve the underlying causes of production losses and associated costs by adopting these advanced technologies.

1. The Role of AI and Machine Learning in Smart Manufacturing

Machine learning and artificial intelligence are significantly influential in the manufacturing sector. The industrial Internet of Things (IoT) and smart factories are generating vast quantities of data, which has led to the emergence of AI solutions as potent instruments for efficient analysis and utilisation.

a) Predictive Maintenance

A notable aspect of AI in the manufacturing sector is predictive maintenance. Manufacturers can enhance their maintenance planning and failure prediction capabilities by incorporating AI algorithms into their production data. The ability of AI to spot trends and abnormalities in data allows for the early identification of equipment failures or malfunctions. Manufacturers can achieve more efficient and cost-effective operations by correctly predicting maintenance requirements, minimising unplanned outages, reducing costly repairs, and optimising maintenance schedules.

b) Demand Forecasting and Inventory Management

In order to optimise inventory management and production planning, it is essential to have precise demand forecasts. Market trends, customer behaviour, historical sales data, and external factors can be analysed using AI techniques such as ML algorithms to produce precise demand forecasts. Manufacturers can eliminate stockouts, minimise excess inventory, and optimise their supply chain operations by optimising inventory levels in accordance with these forecasts. Also, this enhances customer satisfaction and reduces inventory-related expenses.

c) Quality Control and Defect Detection

Manufacturers are required to maintain high product quality to satisfy customers and comply with industry standards. In order to facilitate real-time quality control, AI and ML techniques can be implemented to monitor and analyse data from a variety of sensors, cameras, and inspection systems. AI systems can implement immediate corrective actions by identifying defects, anomalies, or deviations from desirable parameters, thereby minimising waste and guaranteeing consistent product quality.

d) Process Optimisation and Efficiency

Manufacturing processes can be optimised and operational efficiency can be enhanced through the use of AI and ML algorithms. Artificial intelligence systems can analyse data from a variety of sources, including sensor inputs, machine records, and historical performance data, to identify process constraints, optimise production schedules, and improve resource allocation. In turn, this results in cost savings, enhanced productivity, reduced cycle times, and streamlined operations.

e) Human-Machine Collaboration

For smart manufacturing environments to function effectively, human operatives and machines must collaborate seamlessly. By automating hazardous or repetitive jobs, offering real-time insights, and supporting employees in complicated decision-making processes, AI technology may improve teamwork. Cobots, or collaborative robotics, that are outfitted with AI capabilities, can operate in conjunction with humans, thereby enhancing the flexibility, safety, and productivity of the shop floor.

2. AI and ML for MSMEs in Smart Manufacturing

It is imperative to acknowledge the substantial potential and distinctive opportunities that AI and ML in smart manufacturing present for "Micro, Small & Medium Enterprises (MSMEs)," even though the focus has frequently been on large enterprises.

The analysis indicates that the most extensively researched application domains for MSMEs are maintenance and quality. To reduce maintenance costs, optimise equipment availability, and minimise uncertainties in diagnosing machine failures, predictive maintenance solutions have been developed by utilising the capabilities of AI and ML. Furthermore, the automation of defect detection through

AI and ML techniques has become essential for the improvement of product quality, the reduction of human errors, and the enhancement of quality control processes.

AI and ML technologies are also acquiring traction among MSMEs in other sectors. This technology provides substantial advantages in the areas of energy management, robotics, cybersecurity, material handling, supply chain management, and production planning and scheduling. AI and ML are revolutionising the operations of MSMEs in a variety of businesses, from the prediction of energy demand and optimisation of inventory management to the development of customisable robotic manipulators and the enhancement of cybersecurity measures.

3. Limitations and Challenges for MSMEs in Adopting AI/ML in Smart Manufacturing

Despite the significant potential for MSMEs to enhance processes and remain competitive in dynamic markets through the implementation of AI/ML solutions, their pervasive adoption is impeded by a variety of limitations and challenges. The primary challenges that MSMEs encounter when attempting to implement AI/ML technologies in smart manufacturing are as follows:

a) Data problems

Quantity, quality, and availability of data are substantial constraints on the effective application of AI/ML techniques. Structured and automated data capture processes must be implemented to address the insufficient data that many MSMEs have to input into AI/ML models. Furthermore, various application fields have varying dataset availability for model validation, which results in gaps in data accessibility. Data security, transparency, and cybersecurity concerns are also critical considerations for MSMEs.

b) Lack of knowledge and skills

MSMEs frequently encounter a dearth of expertise and knowledge in Information Technology (IT) and AI/ML. This knowledge divide hinders their capacity to completely leverage AI/ML solutions, despite their recognition of their potential advantages. The intricacies of implementing AI/ML may be challenging for MSMEs due to several factors, including staff age, demography, lack of training, and experience.

c) Budget constraints

MSMEs typically operate with restricted budgets for technology investments in comparison to larger organisations. Furthermore, MSMEs hold the belief that the cost of AI/ML solutions is exorbitant, even though this may not always be the case. MSMEs' adoption of AI/ML applications is further hampered by the absence of techniques and resources for precisely estimating the cost-benefit ratio of these technologies.

d) Complexity of solution

AI/ML-based solutions are frequently perceived as excessively intricate in the context of Micro, Small, and

Medium-sized Enterprises (MSMEs). Despite the improvement in the availability of user-friendly tools in recent years, MSMEs continue to encounter challenges in participating in AI/ML initiatives as a result of their limited knowledge and resources. In order to ensure the successful adoption of MSMEs, it is essential to simplify the implementation process and offer solutions that are accessible and customised to their unique needs.

e) Lack of management involvement and strategy

Managers must be involved in comprehending the feasibility and advantages of ML solutions. However, many MSMEs lack defined strategies for data collection and ML utilisation. The prevention of adverse consequences necessitates a gradual and meticulously planned strategy to surmount the entry barriers associated with AI/ML transformation. One of the most significant obstacles that MSMEs face is the necessity of obtaining management buy-in and commitment.

f) Lack of constrained end-to-end solutions

MSMEs are in search of AI/ML solutions that are both simplistic and straightforward to implement. The solutions they require are practical and can be rapidly deployed and integrated into their current architecture. MSMEs are at risk of being left behind as large businesses continue to implement AI/ML applications. There is a need for research to concentrate on the development of frameworks that are tailored to the specific needs of MSMEs and reduce the necessity for extensive technical knowledge.

g) Difficulty in identifying appropriate solutions

The selection of the most appropriate AI/ML-based solutions for specific issues is a substantial challenge for MSMEs. The process entails a thorough comprehension of the fundamental issue, painstaking parameter refining, and extensive data preparation. These sophisticated solutions are seldom encountered in the daily operations of MSMEs, which complicates their evaluation of the applicability and utility of AI/ML technologies.

h) Human-related issues

AI/ML technologies must be successfully implemented with the involvement and consent of employees. Adoption of AI/ML may be greatly impacted by low employee engagement or reluctance to change. For MSMEs, making sure that employees participate, get training, and communicate effectively becomes a crucial problem. Additionally, as repetitive and routinely demanding professions may be replaced by machines, it is necessary to evaluate the influence of automation on employment.

6.4 AI in Supply Chain Optimisation

AI is employed by businesses to manage and optimise supply chain activities, including the identification of fuel-efficient delivery routes, the balancing of inventory levels, and the monitoring of product quality, with a greater degree of efficiency than traditional software.

Applications that replicate human intellect and execute

intricate tasks are collectively referred to as Artificial Intelligence (AI). Machine Learning (ML) is one of its subfields, in which systems acquire knowledge by ingesting massive quantities of data rather than being programmed with sequential instructions. In a variety of applications, including the decoding of information from video broadcasts, the interpretation of spoken and written text, the prediction of future market behaviour, the production of decisions in intricate scenarios, and the surfacing of insights that are concealed within large data sets, AI systems can outperform traditional software.

1. End-to-End Supply Chain Transparency with AI

Manufacturers find it difficult to keep an end-to-end track of the flow of resources and commodities arriving at their facilities because of the complexity, entanglement, and expansion of modern supply chains. Despite the complexity of logistics networks, AI's distinctive capacity to swiftly analyse large data sets can provide insight into their inner workings.

Intelligent algorithms that have been trained through machine learning frequently extract valuable insights, such as the causes of variability or methods for enhancing the capacity of processes with fixed and variable time elements that result in bottlenecks, when they consume massive streams of recorded data and other logistics signals. Furthermore, traditional Supply Chain Management (SCM) systems are inferior to AI-powered

SCM tools in their ability to monitor immense quantities of supplies in real time as they traverse intermediary manufacturing and distribution partners on their journey to becoming finalised products. Suppliers who may be violating ethical or quality procurement practices may be identified by manufacturers through this improved visibility and traceability.

2. Benefits of AI in Supply Chain

Manufacturers have been at the vanguard of AI innovation, experimenting with and deploying a variety of AI technologies across the numerous production facilities, storage and distribution centres, and transport vehicles included in contemporary supply chains. This has the potential to generate multiple benefits:

a) Improved Warehouse Efficiency

AI has the potential to enhance the efficiency of facilities by assisting in the organisation of their racking and the design of their arrangements. Machine learning algorithms may recommend floor plans that expedite inventory access and journey times, from reception to racks to packing and shipping stations, by analysing the volumes of commodities moved through warehouse aisles. Additionally, they can facilitate the planning of optimal routes for robotics and employees to expedite the movement of inventory, thereby increasing fulfilment rates. Further optimising warehouse capacity, AI-enabled forecasting tools assist producers in balancing inventory against carrying costs by analysing demand signals from marketing, manufacturing line, and point-of-sale systems.

b) Reduced Operating Costs

AI's capacity to learn intricate behaviours and operate in unpredictable environments enables the completion of repetitive tasks, including inventory documentation, monitoring, and counting, with increased precision and reduced labour. Additionally, constraints are identified and resolved. A complex supply chain can be operated at a lower cost by AI, which can identify inefficiencies and learn from repetitive tasks.

AI can also reduce the outages of critical equipment, thereby saving manufacturers and distribution administrators money. Intelligent systems, particularly those that process data from IoT devices in smart factories, can anticipate malfunctions and failures in their early phases, thereby reducing disruptions and resulting financial losses.

c) Fewer Errors And Less Waste

In general, AI can identify anomalous behaviour in both humans and machines much more promptly than humans. This is the reason why manufacturers, warehouse operators, and transportation companies are developing algorithms to identify deficiencies in their workflows, employee errors, and product defects. Computer vision systems that employ artificial intelligence to inspect work to minimise recalls, returns, and revisions are fed by cameras deployed in logistics centres, assembly lines, and delivery vehicles.

The system can detect errors made by both workers and machines before the misassembly or shipment of products to the incorrect location, thereby reducing material waste and saving time. Additionally, intelligent systems can perform root cause analysis, which involves the evaluation of extensive data sets to identify correlations that elucidate failings and enable teams to implement more effective solutions more promptly.

AI is also directly integrated into ERP systems that are used to manage financial transactions as products progress through the supply chain, thereby assisting companies in avoiding costly invoicing and payment errors.

d)   More-Accurate Inventory Management

AI's capabilities are being leveraged by manufacturers to optimise their inventory management processes. For instance, forecasting systems that are propelled by AI can assess the demand of a downstream customer by utilising inventory information that has been shared. The manufacturer's demand forecasts will be adjusted by the system if it determines that the customer's demand is decreasing.

Additionally, manufacturers and supply chain managers are increasingly utilising computer vision systems to monitor warehouse storage capacity and tabulate products in real-time. This involves the installation of cameras on supply chain infrastructure, containers, vehicles, and even drones. Furthermore, AI automates the process of creating, amending, and extracting information from inventory documentation, as well as recording these workflows in inventory ledgers.

e)   Optimised Operations Through Simulations

Supply chain managers can conduct AI-powered simulations to acquire a deeper understanding of the operations of intricate, global logistics networks and to identify opportunities for improvement.

Digital twins, which are graphical 3D representations of actual items and processes, such as industrial production lines or completed commodities, are being used in combination with AI more and more. Compared to simulations conducted using conventional computation methods, these simulations are more precise when AI selects the models and manages the workflows. This AI application can assist engineers and production managers in evaluating the effects of redesigning products, replacing components, or implementing new machinery on the factory floor.

In addition to 3D digital duplicates, AI and ML can also assist in the development of 2D visual models of external processes. This enables planners and operations managers to assess the potential effects of moving storage and distribution centres, redirecting shipping and distribution routes, or changing suppliers.

f) Improved Worker And Material Safety

AI systems are capable of monitoring work environments throughout the supply chain, including assembly lines, storage facilities, and transportation vehicles, and can identify conditions that endanger the safety of both workers and the public. For example, computer vision could be employed to enforce the use of personal protective equipment (PPE) or to ensure that employees adhere to other company safety protocols and Occupational Safety and Health Administration standards. Alternatively, it can include analysing information from systems on trucks and forklifts to confirm that drivers are driving them in a sober and safe manner.

AI can assist in the prediction of malfunctions and other potentially hazardous situations when monitoring factory equipment. Additionally, peripheral safety devices that are fuelled by AI can enhance protection. Consider vests that are equipped with sensors and are connected to AI systems. These vests analyse the movements of warehouse workers and notify them of the potential for injury based on their posture, activities, or location within the warehouse.

In addition to safeguarding those who reside and work in the vicinity, AI systems that are informed by sensors in distribution facilities and vehicles also contribute to the proper handling and disposal of hazardous materials. AI can automate hazardous duties, thereby enabling employees to circumvent hazardous situations.

g) More-Timely Deliveries

It is particularly important for manufacturers that assemble products through intricate supply chains to ensure that deliveries are timely and well-coordinated. A single component's delayed arrival can significantly disrupt an entire production schedule. AI is now responsible for reducing these delivery delays.

Machine learning is employed by logistics companies to develop models that optimise and supervise the delivery routes that components traverse throughout the supply chain. These models can prioritise dispatches according to the significance of the consumer, contractual deadlines, order volumes, product availability, or delivery promises. Additionally, they can more precisely predict the arrival timings of all nodes in the distribution network, detecting shipments that might cause more serious issues if they are delayed.

h) Improved Supply Chain Sustainability

AI has the potential to reduce the negative environmental impact of supply chains and increase their sustainability by enhancing operational efficiencies. ML-trained models can assist organisations in reducing energy consumption by optimising truckloads and delivery routes, resulting in a reduction in petroleum consumption while delivering supplies. AI can also assist in the reduction of product waste at various phases of the supply chain. Consider AI-driven production planning, which analyses real-time machine maintenance statuses, current demand forecasts, and past inventory levels to prevent manufacturers from overproducing.

AI is also employed to analyse the lifecycles of completed products and provide insights that support a circular economy, in which materials are recycled and reused. Additionally, supply chain planning and sourcing systems that incorporate AI can increase transparency among suppliers and facilitate their compliance with environmental and social sustainability standards, including the equitable compensation of workers.

i) More-Precise Demand Forecasting

The gold standard for demand prediction is Artificial Intelligence (AI), which takes into account both external signals like economic outlooks, seasonal sales patterns, and larger industry trends, as well as internal data signals like marketing leads and sales pipelines. Supply chain planners may forecast demand and the possible effects of events like economic downturns or extreme weather on demand, as well as on their own costs, manufacturing capacity, and delivery ability, by using AI built into demand planning software.

3. Preparation of Supply Chain for AI

It is frequently difficult and costly for businesses to completely implement AI in production environments.

These measures may be implemented before the identification of a particular project, in certain instances, to optimise a legacy supply chain planning and management system for intelligence enhancement.

a) Audit value creation

Before selecting a specific node in their supply chain to enhance with AI, manufacturers may find it advantageous to conduct an audit of their entire logistics network to identify productivity declines, error-prone processes, and bottlenecks. These audits assist business strategists in determining the most profitable areas for AI and other technology investments.

b) Create a strategy and roadmap

Typically, a supply chain modernisation initiative entails the resolution of numerous issues, the acquisition of numerous benefits, and the satisfaction of executive leaders. However, the majority of manufacturers are unable to afford the cost and disruption associated with upgrading all systems simultaneously.

Before delineating specific initiatives, establish priorities. Subsequently, devise a comprehensive transformation strategy that addresses the most critical issues during its initial phases.

Develop a roadmap that guarantees that each project in the pipeline will facilitate the subsequent one and receive sufficient funding.

c) Design a solution

The solution design process begins after identifying the supply chain operation most suited for AI integration. This involves evaluating required systems, such as cloud applications, servers, data science platforms, and IoT devices, and ensuring their integration with existing IT infrastructure. At this stage, many organisations opt to engage a systems integrator or industry-specific consultancy for expert guidance.

d) Select a vendor

Many technology vendors offer supply chain solutions claiming AI integration, though these capabilities vary widely due to the broad scope of AI. Choosing a vendor is akin to forming a long-term partnership. Manufacturers should carefully assess each vendor's technological capabilities, pricing, support models, and corporate culture, guided by recommendations from their systems integrators.

e) Implementation and integration

The process of implementation and integration commences when a company has chosen a technology vendor. A systems integrator typically collaborates with the vendor and internal IT teams to implement, integrate, and test systems before their deployment into production. Upon its conclusion, the implementation phase typically necessitates a period of employee training and some delay.

Nevertheless, the transition from staging to production can be executed with minimal disruption if it is meticulously planned and executed.

f) Remember change management

Employees who have consistently performed their duties in the same manner for an extended period may experience anxiety regarding change, regardless of whether it is labour-intensive or inefficient. Develop a strategy for the organisation to adopt a new AI-enabled solution before its implementation. The plan should include the following: the benchmarks that executives will use to evaluate the project's success, the productivity benefits the organisation aims to achieve, and the problems or objectives that motivate AI adoption. Communication with workers should be conducted.

g) Monitor and adjust

An AI endeavour is never entirely finished in certain respects. AI is a dynamic technology that is perpetually enhanced through a feedback cycle of monitoring and adjustment. Additionally, teams should test different configurations and gather data that monitors the outcomes to guide future performance improvements, even when AI-enabled systems seem to be functioning well.

6.5   AI for Energy Efficiency in Industry

Energy efficiency has become a cornerstone of industrial sustainability, driven by escalating energy costs and increasing regulatory pressures to reduce carbon emissions. Artificial Intelligence (AI) is emerging as a transformative force in this arena, offering the ability to optimise energy consumption, enhance operational efficiency, and reduce environmental impact. By leveraging machine learning algorithms, predictive analytics, and real-time data processing, industries can address complex energy challenges with precision and agility.

1. The Role of AI in Energy Management

AI plays a multifaceted role in energy efficiency by enabling data-driven decision-making. Through the integration of sensors and IoT devices, industrial operations generate massive amounts of data related to energy consumption, equipment performance, and environmental conditions. AI algorithms analyse this data to identify patterns, anomalies, and optimisation opportunities.

a. **Energy Monitoring and Analysis:** AI-powered systems provide continuous monitoring of energy usage across various processes and facilities. This granular visibility enables companies to pinpoint inefficiencies, such as energy leaks or underperforming equipment. By identifying these issues early, businesses can implement corrective measures to reduce waste.

b. **Predictive Maintenance:** Equipment malfunctions or inefficiencies often lead to excessive energy consumption. AI-based predictive maintenance systems use historical and real-time data to forecast equipment failures before they occur. This proactive approach minimises downtime and ensures that machinery operates at peak efficiency.

c. **Process Optimisation:** Industrial processes often involve complex, interdependent variables. AI optimises these processes by simulating different scenarios and recommending adjustments to parameters such as temperature, pressure, or production speed. These optimisations can result in significant energy savings while maintaining output quality.

2. AI Techniques for Energy Efficiency

Several AI techniques are instrumental in achieving energy efficiency in industry. Each technique has distinct applications and benefits, tailored to specific industrial needs.

a. **Machine Learning (ML):** Machine learning algorithms analyse historical data to predict future energy consumption patterns. These predictions enable industries to adjust operations dynamically, such as shifting high-energy tasks to off-peak hours.

b. **Neural Networks:** Deep learning models, particularly neural networks, excel in recognising complex patterns and dependencies in energy data. These models are used for tasks like load forecasting and anomaly detection, which are crucial for maintaining efficient energy use.

c. **Reinforcement Learning (RL):** Reinforcement learning trains AI agents to make decisions by rewarding energy-efficient behaviours. For instance, RL can optimise the operation of HVAC systems in manufacturing facilities to balance energy use with ambient comfort requirements.

d. **Digital Twins:** A digital twin is a virtual replica of a physical asset or system. AI-powered digital twins simulate industrial operations to predict energy outcomes under different scenarios, allowing companies to experiment with energy-saving strategies without disrupting actual production.

3. Applications of AI in Major Industries

AI-driven energy efficiency solutions are being deployed across various industrial sectors, showcasing their versatility and impact.

a. **Manufacturing:** Manufacturing facilities are among the most energy-intensive operations. AI systems optimise production lines, reduce idle machine time, and ensure that energy-intensive processes operate only when necessary. For example, AI can dynamically adjust robotic assembly lines to minimise power usage without compromising throughput.

b. **Oil and Gas:** In the oil and gas sector, AI improves energy efficiency through enhanced reservoir management, pipeline monitoring, and refining operations. Predictive analytics identify potential inefficiencies, such as pipeline leaks, reducing energy wastage and improving safety.

c. **Chemical Industry:** AI supports the chemical industry by optimising reaction processes, controlling heating and cooling systems, and ensuring consistent product quality. By fine-tuning these variables, energy consumption is significantly reduced.

d. **Automotive:** Automotive manufacturers leverage AI to streamline energy usage in production processes and logistics. Additionally, AI-driven energy management systems in Electric Vehicle (EV) manufacturing optimise battery production, reducing energy waste.

e. **Food and Beverage:** Energy-intensive operations like refrigeration, cooking, and packaging are optimised using AI. Predictive analytics ensure that energy usage aligns with production schedules, minimising waste.

4. Benefits of AI for Energy Efficiency

The adoption of AI for energy efficiency offers numerous benefits, including:

a. **Cost Savings:** By reducing energy consumption, industries significantly lower their utility bills. AI-driven optimisations often result in quick returns on investment.

b. **Environmental Impact:** Reduced energy consumption leads to lower greenhouse gas emissions, helping industries meet sustainability goals and comply with environmental regulations.

c. **Enhanced Productivity:** Energy-efficient operations often correlate with improved productivity. Optimised processes reduce downtime and ensure consistent performance.

d. **Regulatory Compliance:** Governments worldwide are imposing stricter energy efficiency and emissions standards. AI enables industries to adhere to these regulations seamlessly.

CHAPTER 7

AI and ML in Entertainment and Media

Learning Objective

This chapter explores the impact of AI on content personalisation, recommendation systems, video editing, gaming, virtual reality, music and art creation, and sentiment analysis in media.

7.1 AI in Content Personalisation and Recommendation Systems

In the digital age, the sheer volume of content available online has made it challenging for users to find relevant information. This has led to the emergence of content personalisation and recommendation systems, which play a pivotal role in tailoring content to individual user preferences.

At the heart of these systems lies AI, which has revolutionised the way content is curated and delivered. By leveraging machine learning, natural language processing, and deep learning, AI-driven personalisation and recommendation systems have transformed industries ranging from e-commerce and entertainment to education and healthcare.

1. The Evolution of Content Personalisation

Content personalisation is not a new concept. Early forms of personalisation involved basic filtering techniques, such as keyword matching or manual categorisation. However, these methods were limited in scope and often failed to account for the nuances of user preferences.

With the advent of AI, content personalisation has become more sophisticated, enabling systems to analyse vast amounts of data and deliver highly targeted recommendations.

One of the significant milestones in this evolution was the introduction of collaborative filtering. This method leverages user behaviour, such as ratings, clicks, or purchase history, to identify patterns and suggest content based on similarities with other users. Collaborative filtering laid the groundwork for modern AI-driven recommendation systems by highlighting the potential of data-driven insights.

2. The Role of Machine Learning in Recommendation Systems

Machine Learning (ML) is a cornerstone of AI-powered recommendation systems. It enables these systems to learn from data and improve over time without explicit programming. Two primary approaches are commonly used in ML-based recommendation systems: supervised learning and unsupervised learning.

a. **Supervised Learning:** In this approach, models are trained on labelled datasets to predict user preferences. For example, an e-commerce platform might use past purchase data to recommend products to a customer. Algorithms such as decision trees, support vector machines, and neural networks are often employed in supervised learning.

b. **Unsupervised Learning:** This approach involves clustering and association techniques to identify patterns in unstructured data. For instance, clustering algorithms can group users with similar preferences, enabling more accurate recommendations. Principal Component Analysis (PCA) and k-means clustering are popular methods in this category.

Reinforcement learning, a subset of ML, is also gaining traction in recommendation systems. It focuses on optimising long-term user engagement by learning from interactions. For example, streaming platforms like Netflix use reinforcement learning to suggest shows that maximize user retention.

3. Natural Language Processing and Content Understanding

Natural Language Processing (NLP) is another critical component of AI in personalisation and recommendation systems. NLP enables machines to understand, interpret, and generate human language, which is essential for processing textual content.

    a. **Text Analysis**: NLP techniques like sentiment analysis, topic modelling, and named entity recognition help systems analyse user-generated content, such as reviews or comments. This analysis provides valuable insights into user preferences and helps refine recommendations.

    b. **Content Generation**: Advanced NLP models, such as OpenAI's GPT series, can generate personalised content, such as product descriptions or blog posts, tailored to specific user segments.

    c. **Semantic Search**: Traditional keyword-based search often fails to capture the intent behind a query. NLP-powered semantic search bridges this gap by understanding context and delivering more relevant results. This capability is crucial for content recommendation engines in industries like e-learning and news.

4. Deep Learning and Neural Networks

Deep learning, a subset of machine learning, has significantly enhanced the capabilities of recommendation systems. By utilising neural networks, deep learning models can process complex and high-dimensional data, such as images, videos, and text.

    a. **Convolutional Neural Networks (CNNs)**: CNNs are widely used for image and video content recommendation. Platforms like YouTube leverage CNNs to analyse video thumbnails and recommend visually appealing content.

b. **Recurrent Neural Networks (RNNs)**: RNNs excel in processing sequential data, making them ideal for predicting user behaviour over time. For instance, music streaming services use RNNs to create dynamic playlists based on listening history.

c. **Transformers**: Transformer-based models, such as BERT and GPT, have revolutionised NLP tasks by enabling context-aware recommendations. These models are particularly effective in understanding user queries and delivering precise results.

5. **Applications Across Industries**

AI-driven personalisation and recommendation systems have found applications in a wide range of industries, each benefiting from tailored content delivery:

a. **E-commerce**: Personalised product recommendations are a hallmark of e-commerce platforms like Amazon and Flipkart. By analysing user behaviour and preferences, these platforms increase conversion rates and customer satisfaction.

b. **Entertainment**: Streaming services like Netflix and Spotify rely on AI to recommend movies, TV shows, and songs. These systems consider factors such as viewing history, genre preferences, and even time of day to curate personalised experiences.

c. **Education**: E-learning platforms use AI to recommend courses, learning materials, and exercises based on a student's progress and interests. This approach enhances engagement and facilitates personalised learning journeys.

d. **Healthcare**: AI-powered systems in healthcare recommend personalised treatment plans, fitness regimens, and wellness content. For instance, apps like MyFitnessPal suggest diet and exercise routines tailored to individual goals.

e. **News and Media**: News aggregators like Google News employ AI to deliver articles aligned with user interests. By analysing reading habits and preferences, these platforms ensure users stay informed about topics they care about.

7.2 Machine Learning for Video Editing and Production

Today, the significance and relevance of AI in the production and editing of video cannot be exaggerated. Smart technology has emerged as a game-changer, allowing professionals to work more efficiently and creatively in response to the increasing demand for high-quality content and the necessity of meeting strict deadlines. This ground-breaking technology provides video creators with the ability to generate captivating content, expand their audience, and remain competitive in a market that is constantly changing.

1. Explaining AI in Video Production

AI is a type of super-intelligent assistant that is capable of analysing data, learning from it, and making decisions independently in the same way as a human, despite not being a human. The technology in the field of video production adds a touch of enchantment by automating tasks and fostering creativity.

The two pillars of smart technology that are pertinent to filming are as follows:

a) **Machine Learning (ML)**: AI's intelligence allows algorithms to identify patterns and enhance performance without the need for explicit programming. In film production, it can be utilised to automate video editing, identify situations, and even recommend audio that is flawlessly synchronised with the footage.

b) **Computer Vision:** It enables computers to "see" and decipher visual information from pictures and visuals, acting as AI's eyes. Consequently, this technology can be implemented to perform duties such as object tracking, facial recognition, and the identification of particular scenes. Computer vision is employed in AI editing to optimise the workflow and customise it to the content's unique requirements.

It is important to note that AI's entry into the filmmaking industry commenced with fundamental tools that were analogous to ungainly infants who were still in the process of acclimating to their surroundings. However, over time, they have evolved into sophisticated systems capable of managing intricate tasks, such as the automatic generation of highlight videos or the application of stunning visual effects.

Creators and studios equally are enthusiastically integrating smart technology into their operations, as it has been firmly established. AI is more than a passing trend. It has established itself as a permanent fixture in the video production industry, and its integration will only continue to deepen in the years ahead.

2. The Use of AI in Video Production and Editing

In the captivating realm of cinematography, AI delivers exceptional performances in the critical stages of the photography and editing process. Let's review the credits and examine the manner in which it is employed during the different phases of video production.

a) Scriptwriting

AI-driven scriptwriting tools may provide interesting plotlines, character development concepts, and even humorous dialogue by analysing enormous volumes of data. This enhances the creative process and offers invaluable inspiration.

Additionally, the technology can be employed by writers to enhance their scripts by recognising inconsistencies, narrative gaps, and potential enhancements. Furthermore, AI can modify its writing style to align with specific disciplines or emulate the writing of specific authors, thereby enhancing its adaptability and versatility.

b) Subtitling

The transcription of spoken materials and the addition of subtitles to visualisations have been significantly enhanced by intelligent technology. Automated Speech Recognition (ASR) technology is capable of producing transcripts that are highly precise in real-time by accurately converting audio to text.

This not only enhances video production but also facilitates accessibility by providing content to individuals with hearing impairments. Further, intelligent tools can generate multilingual subtitles automatically, thereby broadening the audience for visuals to include international audiences.

c) Voice Acting

Traditionally, the process of producing voiceovers for videos involves the employment of voice actors and the recording of extensive sessions in a studio. The landscape has been substantially altered by AI-driven Text-To-Speech (TTS) technology. In a variety of languages and dialects, creators can transform written compositions into natural-sounding voiceovers with the assistance of high-quality TTS systems. This not only facilitates the localisation of content for global audiences but also saves time and money.

Meanwhile, the accuracy and speed of these systems have been significantly enhanced by intelligent voice and speech recognition technology, which guarantees the seamless synchronisation of audio and video elements.

d) Real-Time Video Analytics

The days of relying on conjecture to evaluate video performance are over. The technology has transformed the process of analysing and comprehending visual materials. AI-powered video analytics can monitor and interpret a variety of metrics, including audience engagement, view time, and click-through rates.

This data assists video producers and marketers in the optimisation of their content, the comprehension of audience preferences, and the refinement of their strategies to achieve superior performance. Creators can gain valuable insights into the emotional response of viewers through AI-driven analytics, which can help them identify the aspects of their materials that resonate most with the audience.

e) Video Editing

Smart technology can analyse video footage, identify critical sequences, and even devise appropriate transitions and visual effects to produce a more refined and engaging final product. AI-powered video editing tools facilitate more efficient post-production workflows and are particularly advantageous for the creation of brief content, such as promotional visualisations and social media clips.

f) Visual Effects

AI is being utilised more frequently to improve the quality of "Computer-Generated Imagery (CGI)" and visual effects in video production. "Generative Adversarial Networks (GANs)" and deep learning algorithms have facilitated the transformation of scenes, characters, and backgrounds with greater ease and speed, resulting in more realistic and remarkable visual effects.

g) Content Moderation

AI-driven content moderation tools are instrumental in the identification and filtering of inappropriate or detrimental content for video platforms and streaming services. By detecting and flagging materials that contravene community guidelines, these systems guarantee a more suitable and secure environment for users.

3. AI Benefits for Video Production

Intelligent technology has the potential to simplify and improve the entire filmmaking process by implementing innovative solutions and remarkable advancements.

a) Efficiency and Time Optimisation

AI-driven editing tools can slice and carve footage in record time due to their capacity to analyse and process data rapidly. Video producers are now afforded additional time to refine their materials, as tasks that previously required hours can now be completed in minutes. AI emerges as the dependable assistant you have always desired when it comes to performing mundane and repetitive duties. It can autonomously manage time-consuming tasks such as organising media assets, transcription, and video labelling. Raw footage analysis, scene detection, highlight identification, and the generation of a first-cut edit are all capabilities of intelligent algorithms.

AI-enabled video summarization is capable of effectively extracting key moments and generating concise summaries in situations where extensive videos must be condensed. This feature is especially beneficial for social media platforms, event coverage, and news channels, where conciseness is essential. This automation frees up a significant amount of time for creators and editors, allowing them to concentrate on more thrilling aspects of their projects.

b) Enhanced Creativity

By examining historical data, user preferences, and trends, intelligent models can generate innovative content ideas. This can be a valuable resource for creators who are interested in discovering latent audience interests or pursuing new inspiration.

Visual effects are elevated to new heights by AI's aptitude

for computer vision. It can seamlessly incorporate CGI elements into live-action footage, generate breathtaking animations, and apply distinctive filters to achieve a unique visual style. This presents a plethora of opportunities for captivating storytelling that captivates the imaginations of viewers.

c) Personalisation

AI enables video producers to generate customised content experiences for each observer. The technology can enhance user engagement and contentment by suggesting customised visuals based on audience behaviour, preferences, and engagement patterns. Adverts, product recommendations, and entire video compilations can all be personalised to enhance the viewing experience and ensure that it is pertinent to the particular observer.

d) Cost Reduction and Accessibility

AI's efficacy results in cost savings. The automation of duties and the optimisation of procedures can result in a substantial decrease in production expenses. This democratises the video production landscape, enabling the production of high-quality content on a budget of any size.

Smart technology enables creators and smaller teams to access sophisticated editing and production tools by levelling the playing field. Creative minds with restricted resources can now generate professional-looking visuals without incurring significant expenses.

4. AI Limitations in Video Production

Although AI has significantly altered the field of video production, it still has some limitations in terms of emotional intelligence and creativity:

a) **Lack of creative intuition**: Despite its ability to analyse and process large datasets with ease, the technology continues to struggle to understand the complexities of human emotions, artistic vision, and storytelling. Creativity frequently necessitates the ability to make intuitive decisions and consider outside the box, which AI is unable to accurately replicate.

b) **Adaptability**: Data and training packages are indispensable components of intelligent technology utilised in video production. In the presence of sufficient data, it can perform exceptionally well in specific duties; however, it may become impeded when confronted with novel or intricate situations. Real-time decision-making, contextual comprehension, and adaptability continue to be substantial obstacles for intelligent systems.

c) **Emotional and ethical considerations**: Intelligent Filmmaking instruments are deficient in ethical awareness and emotional intelligence. They may not understand the possible repercussions of their work or how viewers are affected by delicate material. For instance, an AI algorithm may generate an aesthetically pleasing scene that unintentionally reinforces detrimental stereotypes or induces emotional distress in viewers.

d) **Authenticity and human connection**: The success of a visual is contingent upon the presence of these elements. However, AI is unable to completely replicate genuine emotions, connections, and relationships, despite its ability to simulate human-like interactions to a certain extent.

e) **Aesthetic judgment**: The process of video production frequently entails the application of subjective aesthetic judgements that are influenced by the unique styles of respective individuals or brands. Smart models may encounter difficulty in comprehending the implications of an organisation's distinctive visual identity or the subtleties of a particular director's style, as they are dependent on historical data.

In order to maintain authenticity in videos, ensure ethical content, cultivate human connections, and stretch the boundaries of creativity, human input is still necessary in some form. Through the integration of AI's capabilities with human producer's creative processes, the industry may reach its maximum potential and develop visually striking, compelling, and emotionally impactful content.

7.3 AI in Gaming and Virtual Reality

Interactive entertainment undergoes a significant transformation with the incorporation of AI and Virtual Reality into gaming experiences. Artificial Intelligence and

Virtual Reality have each revolutionised distinct industries; however, their convergence in gaming has unleashed new dimensions. AI algorithms improve player experiences by producing intelligent NPCs and establishing dynamic environments. Virtual Reality provides users with interactive gameplay and realistic simulations, enveloping them in a virtual world. AI and VR collaborate to redefine the limits of gaming, generating immersive and captivating experiences that obfuscate the distinction between the real and virtual worlds.

1. The Convergence of AI and VR in Modern Gaming

The gaming industry has undergone a significant transformation as a result of the incorporation of Virtual Reality (VR) and Artificial Intelligence (AI). AI improves gaming experiences by generating realistic game environments, adaptive gameplay, and genuine characters. Conversely, VR elevates gaming to a new level by providing immersive and interactive experiences. Modern gaming has been transformed by the convergence of AI and VR, which has revolutionised the development and play of games. This convergence has opened up a world of possibilities.

a) The Emergence of AI in Enhancing Gaming Experiences

Gaming experiences have been transformed by AI, which has emerged as a game-changer. AI algorithms are employed by developers to generate intelligent Non-

Player Characters (NPCs) that adjust to player behaviour, thereby improving the overall realism and immersion of games. NPCs may now engage with players in real-time and provide individualised challenges and experiences thanks to technology that goes beyond conventionally programmed replies.

Moreover, interactive experiences are elevated to new heights by AI-driven virtual characters, which are capable of recognising voice commands and engaging in natural language conversations. The significant impact of AI on the gaming industry is a testament to its critical role in determining its future, as it has the potential to revolutionise gameplay dynamics and player engagement.

b) Virtual Reality: A New Dimension in Interactive Gaming

In interactive gaming experiences, Virtual Reality (VR) introduces a new era that is both immersive and transformative. Virtual reality elevates the level of immersion and authenticity in gaming by seamlessly incorporating participants into virtual environments. To generate dynamic and realistic scenarios that react to player behaviour in real-time, game developers implement AI algorithms in VR environments.

VR gaming transcends conventional gameplay by providing users with the opportunity to investigate novel environments and narratives. VR game development promises consumers unparalleled experiences that obscure the line between the virtual and real worlds, thanks to advancements in AI and object recognition. User experiences in the game business are drastically changing as a result of the confluence of AI and VR.

2. AI Integration in Game Development

The industry has been transformed by the integration of AI in game development. AI algorithms are employed to generate dynamic game content, devise realistic game environments, and construct convincing Non-Player Characters (NPCs). Game developers can now create games that are more immersive, dynamic, and genuine than ever before with the help of AI. The development of games has been revolutionised by AI, which has expanded the boundaries of what is feasible in virtual environments.

a) Crafting Intelligent Non-Player Characters (NPCs) with AI

In any game, Non-Player Characters (NPCs) are essential, as they contribute to the realism and profundity of the virtual world. It is now possible for game developers to construct intelligent NPCs that improve the gameplay experience through the incorporation of AI. AI algorithms analyse player behaviour and adjust NPC behaviour accordingly, resulting in more immersive and unpredictable interactions with NPCs. The following are several critical aspects to emphasise regarding the development of intelligent Non-Player Characters (NPCs) with artificial intelligence:

i. AI-driven NPCs can modify their conduct in real time by learning from user actions.

ii. A dynamic and engaging experience is generated by the ability of NPCs to respond to various gameplay scenarios.

iii. As the game goes on, AI lets NPCs grow and change, which makes interactions more realistic.

iv. Intelligent NPCs contribute to the virtual world's depth and authenticity, thereby improving the overall gameplay experience.

The creation of NPCs has been transformed by the incorporation of AI in game development, resulting in a new level of immersion and intelligence in games. As a result of the presence of sentient NPCs, the game world becomes more interactive and alive, allowing players to have distinct and personalised experiences.

b) Leveraging AI for Realistic and Dynamic Game Environments

Artificial intelligence is essential in the development of dynamic and realistic game environments in contemporary gaming. The realism and immersion of virtual environments have been significantly improved by AI algorithms, which have revolutionised modern game development. By utilising AI, game developers can incorporate dynamic elements into environments that respond to player behaviour, thereby enhancing the overall appeal of the experience.

AI advances the limits of gaming realism by contributing to the authenticity of virtual landscapes through content generation and object recognition. The way games are made and played has changed significantly as a result of these developments in AI technology, bringing in a new age of immersive and engaging gaming experiences for players everywhere. By utilising AI in-game environments, there are limitless opportunities to elevate the level of realism in gaming.

3. Strategic Advantages of VR in Gaming

Virtual Reality (VR) facilitates strategic advantages in gaming by immersing participants in a sensory-rich and completely interactive environment. Game developers can provide players with unparalleled levels of engagement and realism by incorporating VR technology. VR facilitates experiences that surpass conventional gaming, enabling the development of novel gameplay mechanics and narrative techniques.

VR is a critical element in the development of the future of gaming due to the improved user experiences that result from these advancements. The capacity to immerse players in a virtual world, where they can engage with characters and environments in a realistic manner, enhances the quality of gaming experiences. The strategic advantage of VR is its ability to transform how games are played and experienced, thereby creating new opportunities for the gaming industry.

a) Immersive Learning: The Role of VR in Educational Games

Virtual reality has a substantial impact on the development of educational games, providing immersive learning experiences that surpass conventional teaching methods. Several critical aspects should be emphasised:

i.   VR offers a learning environment that is immersive and has the potential to engage students, thereby improving their educational experiences.

ii. The VR integration education enables students to engage with virtual objects and environments, thereby enhancing the hands-on nature of the learning experience.

iii. The use of VR in educational games provides students with a secure and regulated environment in which to experiment with a variety of concepts.

iv. Through immersive and interactive learning experiences, VR improves critical thinking skills and spatial awareness.

The purpose of VR in educational games is to transform the manner in which students interact with educational content and acquire knowledge. VR offers educational institutions the opportunity to establish interactive and engaging learning environments by offering immersive learning experiences.

b) VR and Integrated Graphics: Pushing the Limits of Visual Fidelity

Virtual reality gaming is significantly reliant on incorporated graphics to stretch the boundaries of visual fidelity. The integration of integrated graphics with VR technology generates breathtaking visuals that envelop participants in virtual worlds that are both convincing and realistic. Several significant aspects should be emphasised:

i. The rendering of realistic textures, lighting effects, and visual details is facilitated by the integration of graphics in VR gaming.

ii. The player's perception of immersion and presence in the virtual world is heightened by the visual fidelity of VR gaming.

iii. Integrated graphics are designed to enhance performance and guarantee a seamless gaming experience in virtual reality environments.

iv. Visual fidelity is an essential component of VR game design, as it enhances the overall immersive and genuine experience.

The convergence of VR and integrated graphics in gaming is establishing a new era of visually captivating and immersive gameplay experiences. VR gaming with incorporated graphics redefines the limits of visual fidelity, generating captivating virtual worlds that captivate players.

7.4   AI for Music and Art Creation

The world of creative arts is no exception to the global transformation of industries by Artificial Intelligence (AI). AI technologies are expanding the boundaries of what is feasible, enabling inventive partnerships between human creators and machines in a variety of fields, including music composition and fine art creation. The impact of AI on the authenticity of human-made art is a matter of concern for some, as some regard it as a potent instrument for enhancing creativity.

1.   The Evolution of AI in Music

In recent years, the impact of AI on music has expanded significantly, as machine learning and neural networks have enabled the development of more advanced music composition and production tools. The role of AI in music is not a recent development; it began with basic algorithms that could generate melodies. However, AI has since evolved to the point where it can compose entire albums, combine recordings, and even replicate the techniques of renowned composers and musicians.

a)   AI-Assisted Composition

Composition is one of the most notable domains in which AI is revolutionising the music industry. AI platforms, including AIVA (Artificial Intelligence Virtual Artist) and OpenAI's MuseNet, are capable of producing intricate compositions in a diverse array of musical genres. For example, MuseNet can employ deep learning techniques to compose music in the styles of Mozart or Chopin, as well as in more contemporary genres such as jazz and pop. This form of AI support enables musicians to explore novel noises and concepts that may not have been feasible in the absence of AI.

In contrast, AIVA has been employed to compose classical music and is acknowledged as a composer by music rights societies. It has collaborated with human musicians to produce symphonies that combine AI-generated music with human performance, thereby eliciting enquiries regarding authorship and creativity.

b) AI in Music Production and Mixing

The production and harmonising aspects of music are also being transformed by AI. The mastering process is automated by tools such as LANDR, which utilise AI to enable musicians to instantaneously produce professional-sounding recordings. This democratises access to high-quality music production, which was previously exclusively available to individuals with costly equipment or studio access.

Amper Music is another noteworthy advancement that enables musicians to work with AI to produce royalty-free music for a variety of applications, including film scores and video game soundtracks. Amper assists in the development of original music that is customised to meet the specific requirements of the user by allowing them to alter genres, instruments, and tempos.

c) Deep Learning and Music Generation

Artificial intelligence has reached a new level of music generation with the advent of deep learning. Neural networks are currently being investigated by researchers for their potential to produce music that is emotionally charged. AI tools are capable of analysing extant compositions, comprehending their emotional nuance, and composing new pieces that elicit comparable emotions. This has resulted in the utilisation of AI-generated music in therapeutic environments, including the creation of AI-generated soundscapes for relaxation or the creation of soothing compositions for mental health applications.

2. AI in Fine Art: From Creation to Curation

The art world is also experiencing a surge of AI-driven transformation, which encompasses the curation of exhibits, the development of new art forms, and the provision of personalised art experiences.

As AI becomes more incorporated into artistic processes, it is altering the understanding of artistic authorship and creativity.

a) AI-Generated Art

AI's capacity to generate visual art has garnered significant attention, particularly in conjunction with platforms such as DeepArt and DALL·E. These tools generate original works of art by employing Generative Adversarial

Networks (GANs) to analyse extensive datasets of existing art styles. GANs function by training two neural networks: one generates the artwork, while the other critiques it, thereby enhancing the output with each iteration. This technology has resulted in the creation of surreal and breathtaking artworks that challenge conventional conceptions of creativity.

b) Collaborations between AI and Human Artists

AI is evolving into a collaborative partner in the creative process, not just a tool to generate solitary work. In a world where machines can create works that mimic human-made art, working together often blurs the line between human and machine-generated creativity, prompting consideration of the role of the artist.

Similarly, AI-driven tools such as Runway ML offer artists intuitive methods for incorporating AI into their creative productivity, allowing them to experiment with styles and concepts that they may not have previously had the opportunity to investigate.

c) AI as an Art Curator

AI is not only contributing to the creation of art but also to the curating and personalisation of art experiences. Arthena and other platforms employ artificial intelligence to forecast the future value of artworks and analyse market trends. This has implications for both collectors and galleries, as AI-driven insights enable more informed decision-making when purchasing and selling art.

7.5   Sentiment Analysis for Media and Public Opinion

In the digital age, the surge in information availability has transformed the way media and public opinion are shaped. Amid this evolution, Artificial Intelligence (AI) has emerged as a pivotal tool, revolutionising sentiment analysis and offering profound insights into public discourse. By leveraging advanced algorithms and machine learning models, AI enables the efficient processing and interpretation of large volumes of textual, visual, and auditory data.

1.   The Role of Sentiment Analysis in Understanding Public Opinion

Sentiment analysis also referred to as opinion mining, involves extracting and analysing subjective information from data sources. Its objective is to gauge the emotional tone behind content, ranging from positive to neutral to negative. In the context of media and public opinion, sentiment analysis serves as a barometer for understanding societal trends, public reactions, and the emotional underpinnings of major events.

Public opinion plays a crucial role in shaping decisions across sectors, from government policies to corporate strategies. With the rise of social media platforms, traditional surveys and opinion polls have become less effective in capturing the dynamic nature of societal sentiments. AI-powered sentiment analysis bridges this gap by providing real-time, scalable insights into how individuals and communities perceive issues, products, or personalities.

2. Methodologies in AI-Powered Sentiment Analysis

AI employs a variety of methodologies to conduct sentiment analysis. These methods can be broadly classified into rule-based, machine learning-based, and hybrid approaches.

a) Rule-Based Approaches

Rule-based systems rely on pre-defined linguistic rules and lexicons to identify sentiment-laden words or phrases. For instance, words like "excellent" or "horrible" are inherently associated with positive or negative sentiments. While rule-based methods are relatively straightforward and interpretable, they often struggle to capture nuanced expressions, sarcasm, or cultural idioms.

b) Machine Learning-Based Approaches

Machine learning models, particularly those employing Natural Language Processing (NLP), have significantly enhanced the accuracy of sentiment analysis. Techniques such as Support Vector Machines (SVM), Naïve Bayes, and deep learning models like Recurrent Neural Networks (RNNs) and Transformers (e.g., BERT, GPT) allow AI to understand context, detect sentiment polarity, and even predict emotional intensity.

c) Hybrid Approaches

Hybrid models combine rule-based and machine-learning techniques to achieve a balance between interpretability and sophistication. These systems leverage linguistic rules to provide foundational sentiment analysis while enhancing accuracy through machine learning algorithms trained on vast datasets.

3. Applications in Media

The media industry has been a significant beneficiary of AI-driven sentiment analysis. By monitoring audience sentiment, media organisations can tailor content, respond to crises, and gauge the impact of their narratives.

a) Real-Time Social Media Monitoring

AI tools enable media outlets to track social media platforms for trending topics, public sentiment, and audience engagement. By analysing hashtags, comments, and shares, organisations gain insights into societal moods and emerging issues, allowing for timely and relevant reporting.

b) Audience Segmentation and Personalisation

Media companies can utilize sentiment analysis to segment audiences based on emotional responses and preferences. This segmentation allows for personalised content delivery, improving user engagement and satisfaction.

c) Crisis Management

In the age of instant information, crises can escalate rapidly. AI-driven sentiment analysis helps media outlets and organisations detect negative sentiment spikes, enabling prompt responses to mitigate reputational damage.

d) Content Evaluation

Content producers can evaluate the emotional impact of their stories or advertisements through sentiment analysis. By understanding viewer reactions, creators can refine their messaging to better resonate with their target audience.

4. Applications in Public Opinion Analysis

Sentiment analysis is equally transformative in the realm of public opinion, influencing politics, policymaking, and market research.

a) Political Campaigns

Political parties and candidates leverage AI-driven sentiment analysis to gauge voter sentiments, refine messaging, and predict election outcomes. By analysing social media, news coverage, and survey data, campaigns gain a comprehensive understanding of public priorities and concerns.

b) Policy Development

Governments use sentiment analysis to assess public opinion on proposed policies or social initiatives. AI tools enable policymakers to identify potential backlash or areas of support, ensuring more informed and responsive decision-making.

c) Market Research

Corporations rely on sentiment analysis to understand consumer preferences, brand perception, and competitor strategies. By interpreting customer feedback, reviews, and social media conversations, businesses can refine their products and marketing strategies to better align with consumer needs.

d) Crisis Prediction and Management

Beyond immediate crises, sentiment analysis can predict long-term societal shifts or emerging issues. For example, sustained negative sentiment toward a particular issue may indicate the potential for social unrest or public protests, enabling pre-emptive action.

References

[1]. Artificial general intelligence: Russell & Norvig (2021, pp. 32–33, 1020–1021)

[2]. Proposal for the modern version: Pennachin & Goertzel (2007)

[3]. Warnings of overspecialization in AI from leading researchers: Nilsson (1995), McCarthy (2007), Beal & Winston (2009)

[4]. Dartmouth workshop: Russell & Norvig (2021, p. 18), McCorduck (2004, pp. 111–136), NRC (1999, pp. 200–201)

[5]. Successful programs of the 1960s: McCorduck (2004, pp. 243–252), Crevier (1993, pp. 52–107), Moravec (1988, p. 9), Russell & Norvig (2021, pp. 19–21)

[6]. First AI Winter, Lighthill report, Mansfield Amendment: Crevier (1993, pp. 115–117), Russell & Norvig (2021, pp. 21–22), NRC (1999, pp. 212–213), Howe (1994), Newquist (1994, pp. 189–201)

[7]. Second AI Winter: Russell & Norvig (2021, p. 24), McCorduck (2004, pp. 430–435), Crevier (1993, pp. 209–210), NRC (1999, pp. 214–216), Newquist (1994, pp. 301–318)

[8]. Deep learning revolution, AlexNet: Goldman (2022), Russell & Norvig (2021, p. 26), McKinsey (2018)

[9]. Uncertain reasoning: Russell & Norvig (2021, chpt. 12–18), Poole, Mackworth & Goebel (1998, pp. 345–

395), Luger & Stubblefield (2004, pp. 333–381), Nilsson (1998, chpt. 7–12)

[10]. Intractability and efficiency and the combinatorial explosion: Russell & Norvig (2021, p. 21)

[11]. Psychological evidence of the prevalence of sub-symbolic reasoning and knowledge: Kahneman (2011), Dreyfus & Dreyfus (1986), Wason & Shapiro (1966), Kahneman, Slovic & Tversky (1982)

[12]. Thomason, James (21 May 2024). "Mojo Rising: The resurgence of AI-first programming languages". VentureBeat. Archived from the original on 27 June 2024. Retrieved 26 May 2024.

[13]. Wodecki, Ben (5 May 2023). "7 AI Programming Languages You Need to Know". AI Business. Archived from the original on 25 July 2024. Retrieved 5 October 2024.

[14]. Plumb, Taryn (18 September 2024). "Why Jensen Huang and Marc Benioff see 'gigantic' opportunity for agentic AI". VentureBeat. Archived from the original on 5 October 2024. Retrieved 4 October 2024.

[15]. Davenport, T; Kalakota, R (June 2019). "The potential for artificial intelligence in healthcare". Future Healthc J. 6 (2): 94–98. doi:10.7861/futurehosp.6-2-94. PMC 6616181. PMID 31363513.

[16]. Sindhu V, Nivedha S, Prakash M (February 2020). "An Empirical Science Research on Bioinformatics in Machine Learning". Journal of Mechanics of

Continua and Mathematical Sciences (7). doi:10.26782/jmcms.spl.7/2020.02.00006.

[17]. Sarle, Warren S. (1994). "Neural Networks and statistical models". SUGI 19: proceedings of the Nineteenth Annual SAS Users Group International Conference. SAS Institute. pp. 1538–50. ISBN 9781555446116. OCLC 35546178.

[18]. Russell, Stuart; Norvig, Peter (2003) [1995]. Artificial Intelligence: A Modern Approach (2nd ed.). Prentice Hall. ISBN 978-0137903955.

[19]. Langley, Pat (2011). "The changing science of machine learning". Machine Learning. 82 (3): 275–9. doi:10.1007/s10994-011-5242-y.

[20]. Mahoney, Matt. "Rationale for a Large Text Compression Benchmark". Florida Institute of Technology. Retrieved 5 March 2013.

[21]. Bzdok, Danilo; Altman, Naomi; Krzywinski, Martin (2018). "Statistics versus Machine Learning". Nature Methods. 15 (4): 233–234. doi:10.1038/nmeth.4642. PMC 6082636. PMID 30100822.

[22]. Michael I. Jordan (2014-09-10). "statistics and machine learning". reddit. Archived from the original on 2017-10-18. Retrieved 2014-10-01.

[23]. Hung et al. Algorithms to Measure Surgeon Performance and Anticipate Clinical Outcomes in Robotic Surgery. JAMA Surg. 2018

About The Author

Mr. Rakesh Densel holds a **B.Tech in Computer Science Engineering** from **RGPV University, Bhopal,** and has a deep interest in technology and innovation. With **over three years of experience in technical writing,** he has contributed to **more than 20 books** focused on **Artificial Intelligence and Machine Learning.** His writing simplifies complex topics, making them accessible to readers of all levels.

Inspired by his love for technology and computer science, Rakesh created this book to showcase how AI and ML are transforming industries and everyday life. His goal is to help readers understand the practical applications of these powerful technologies.

Outside of writing, Rakesh enjoys playing **chess** and is a passionate advocate for **disability awareness.** As someone with a **physical handicap in both legs,** he believes in overcoming challenges through knowledge and determination. This book reflects his commitment to making AI and ML education inclusive and impactful.